# ALL PRAISE TO THE ALMIGHTY

D0954161

# Vinegar

*The User Friendly
Standard Text, Reference And Guide
To
Appreciating, Making, and
Enjoying Vinegar*

*Lawrence J. Diggs*

*The Only Way to Improve a Good Wine
Is
To Make A Great Vinegar*

*L.J. Diggs
(AKA) The Vinegar Man*

Authors Choice Press
San Jose  New York  Lincoln  Shanghai

**Vinegar**
The User Friendly Standard Text Reference and Guide to
Appreciating, Making, and Enjoying Vinegar.

All Rights Reserved © 1989, 2000 by Lawrence J. Diggs

No part of this book may be reproduced or transmitted in any form or by any
means, graphic, electronic, or mechanical, including photocopying, recording,
taping, or by any information storage or retrieval system, without the
permission in writing from the publisher.

Authors Choice Press
an imprint of iUniverse.com, Inc.

For information address:
iUniverse.com, Inc.
5220 S 16th, Ste. 200
Lincoln, NE 68512
www.iuniverse.com

Originally published by Quiet Storm Publication

ISBN: 0-595-14716-X

Printed in the United States of America

# WHAT PEOPLE ARE SAYING ABOUT THIS BOOK

At last a really complete and detailed exposition of the art and science of vinegar making! This book will create a new home and food crafting hobby. It answered questions I've been asking for years. Thank you Lawrence Diggs.

Jay Conners
Great Fermentations,
San Rafael California
Former president
Home Wine and Beer Trade Association

Thank you for the opportunity to review your book. I really enjoyed reading it and I think it will be very helpful to both the home vinegar maker as well as to the professional large volume vinegar makers. This book is needed and you have done well to fill the need. I will want to buy a copy for each of our managers when you publish.

Donald T. McIntyre
Vice president, Manufacturing
Fleischmann's Vinegar
Alameda, California

I have now read through the draft copy of Vinegar which you recently sent me and I have also asked my colleague Mr.. M.R. Kimmitt (who is a microbiologist at the factory here) to give his comments. The production section seems easily readable to myself and Mr. Kimmitt, and I would not think that anyone with a slight scientific interest would have any problem understanding and digesting the contents.

W.R.J. Evans
Technical Development Manager
H. P. Foods Limited
England

# TABLE OF CONTENTS

## SECTION ONE

## APPRECIATING VINEGAR

### CHAPTER 1
### THE CULTURAL HISTORY
PAGE 19

Reviews and documents the role of vinegar in various cultures throughout the world from ancient times to the present in cultures from Africa to Asia to Europe.

### CHAPTER 2
### THE LEGAL HISTORY
PAGE 41

Reviews and documents the legal history of vinegar. Using the British legal controversy about what constitutes real vinegar, it explains the current legal definition of vinegar. Discusses the connection between scientific discoveries and the legal definitions.

## CHAPTER 3
## THE PRODUCTION HISTORY
### PAGE 49

Discusses the development of technologies for making vinegar. Reveals how scientific discoveries in biology influenced changes in production techniques.


# SECTION TWO

## MAKING VINEGAR

## CHAPTER 4
## UNDERSTANDING THE PROCESS
### PAGE 71

Explains the biological process of vinegar production. Discusses the microorganisms which produce vinegar and the "mother" of vinegar. Looks at the various materials which vinegar can be made from, bacteria nutrients and the physical environment necessary for the bacteria to make vinegar. Reveals various methods for making, testing, aging and storing vinegar.

## CHAPTER 5
## PRODUCTION OF VINEGAR STOCK
### PAGE 121

Illustrates how to make alcohol for the production of vinegar.

## CHAPTER 6
## MAKING VINEGAR
### PAGE 133

Illustrates step by step how to make vinegar using various methods. Reveals the advantages and disadvantages of these methods

## CHAPTER 7
## POST PRODUCTION VINEGARS
### PAGE 155

Illustrates many ways to alter the flavor of vinegar. Discusses flavoring, scenting and blending.

## CHAPTER 8
## TROUBLE SHOOTING
### PAGE 159

Offers methods of detecting and curing the many problems which arise when making vinegar.

## CHAPTER 9
## BALSAMIC VINEGAR
### PAGE 171

Takes a close look at one of the premium vinegars. Explains what makes it so special and how it is made.

## SECTION THREE

## ENJOYING VINEGAR

## CHAPTER 10
## FOOD USES
### PAGE 181

Takes a close look at how important vinegar is in food production. Offers a few unique recipes and ways to use vinegar in food preparation.

## CHAPTER 11
## MEDICAL USES
### PAGE 211

(Humans) Examines the use of vinegar as medicine from ancient times to the present. Documents its use world wide as a medicine. List cures of human ailments attributed to vinegar.

(Other Animals) Looks at how vinegar is used for animals. Lists some cures attributed to vinegar.

## CHAPTER 12
## GENERAL USES
### PAGE 233

Lists many household uses for vinegar other than those in the previous chapters.

## CHAPTER 13
## POP AND SUPERSTITION
### PAGE 246

Vinegar trivia including how vinegar is said in many languages from Arabic to Zulu.

## CHAPTER 14
## VINEGAR AS A HOBBY
### PAGE 253

Offers some of the many ways to enjoy vinegar as a hobby. Includes a discussion on investing, vinegar tasting parties and vinegar contests.

# APPENDICES

## THE END
FOR NOW

# ACKNOWLEDGEMENTS

Thank you for buying and reading this book

Books of this kind cannot be written by one man. It takes the combined efforts of many people, each of them contributing an indispensable part. A writer such as myself merely tries to put together their efforts in a new form.

There have been many people who have studied vinegar and have made important contributions to our understanding of it. Many of their names appear throughout this book and still many more have escaped mention. My sincere thanks to all of them for the many years of labor that they have contributed.

But there are those special people whose advice, technical assistance, encouragement and smiles have helped me through the three years it took me to research and write this book. They deserve special mention.

Amy Beth Banford at the Pfizer Central Research Facility for the electron micrographs of the Acetobaters. Great job!

Bob Beaman at Frings America for help in the understanding of the Frings acetator process and the use of diagrams and photos to explain it.

Chef Luigi Vinegar Company for showing me their unique system for making premium vinegar.

Chris Houston and his "raggae band" for working so hard on the sound track for the hit single "Here Comes the Vinegar Man"

Chuck Lenatti, my editor for helping to make sense out of all of this and make all of this make sense.

Dante Bagnani of American Foods for a lot of help, time and encouragement. The benefits of his help can be seen throughout the entire book.

David Quan for so much patience in teaching me how to use the computer. A real human computer whiz of the first degree.

Deborah Clayton and the University of Alabama for the fine electron micrographs of the vinegar fly.

Dominican college in San Rafael for the use of their photomicrographic equipment.

Don McIntyre and Dick Keeley of Fleishmans Vinegar for help in locating reference material as well as valuable encouragement.

Dr. Hideo Yonenaka, Dr. Anthony Catena, Dr. Greg Antipa and Dr. Frank Bayless at San Francisco State University for help and advice on the difficult questions on the acetobacters.

Dr. Richard Hunderfund, for so much time and encouragement as my advisor in microbiology at San Francisco State University.

Earl "the pearl" Simm, Marion Elliot, Alex Bernoth, Greg Lum and Marilyn Tierney in the San Francisco State University biology stockroom for their help in selecting the right equipment for my experiments.

James Shigley Phd. Director of Research at the Gemnological Society for help in resolving the Cleopatra and the pearl riddle.

Jay Connors at Great Fermentations in Larkspur, California, for the encouragement I needed to write this book.

Ken Sakamoto at Scott Labs for help in isolating and developing cultures of acetobactors.

Kimberly Vinegar Works in San Francisco for explaning to me their unique system for making premium vinegar using the Orleans method.

Krishna Copy Service, the friendliest copy and computer service anywhere, and they really know what they are doing.

Larry and Sandy Davenport and Jane Mc Donald at the Vinegar Institute for many hours of help in researching this book.

Livio Parola for translating the Italian documents.

Macintosh computers for creating a computer powerful enough to write and lay out a book, yet simple enough to be used by a computer idiot.

Michael Hand for translating the German manuscripts.

Microsoft Word for creating a word processing program powerful enough to write and lay out a book, yet simple enough to be used by a computer idiot.

Miki Ichiyanagi for translating the Japanese documents.

Nancy Benson for help in reading the electron micrographs.

Paul and the other fine folks at the San Francisco Public Library for hundreds of hours of research assistance and encouragement over the years it took to research this book.

Reese Vaughn Phd. ,University of California Davis, retired, for his time and kindness in explaining many details about the metabolism of the acetobacter.

Ron Sugiyama for doing the final proofreading. If there are typos I probably put them in after he cleaned it up.

Sally Jones, my first microbiology teacher. Her excitement about microorganisms infected me and indirectly led to writing this book.

San Francisco Municipal Railway (The MUNI )management for being flexible in scheduling my work hours to allow me time to write. And to the members of Local 250A, the transit operators union, for the many kind words of encouragement when the project seemed too big for me.

Scott Zuniga of American Foods for a guided tour and explanation of their modern vinegar plant as well as their Orleans operation.

I pray I have not left out anyone, but so many people have helped me that it is difficult to believe that someone's name has not slipped thru the cracks. My apologies.

# INTRODUCTION

Vinegar is one of the most common, yet unique and wonderful, substances known to mankind.

Think for a moment. What other substance can you name that can be found on the shelves of kitchens all over the world and in small villages as well as large cities? What else can be used almost irrespective of cultural or religious belief, as food, medicine, beauty aid, cleaner, and preservative? And finally, what other substance with all its uses, complexities and varieties can be simply, safely and economically made at home? I know of none except vinegar.

This book will attempt to cover the subject of vinegar well enough to live up to its title "VINEGAR, The standard text and reference and guide etc." To keep the book as exciting as vinegar itself, much of the scientific jargon has been distilled away. That which remains is quite necessary to truly understand vinegar. Many photos and diagrams have been included to make it even more enjoyable.

Your comments to the publisher will be greatly appreciated. This book was written for you.

# SECTION ONE

## APPRECIATING VINEGAR

This section is about the history and folklore of vinegar. It will cover many of the aspects of vinegar that have made it so exciting throughout history. It will also demonstrate and document its place in the development of human cultures from ancient to modern times.

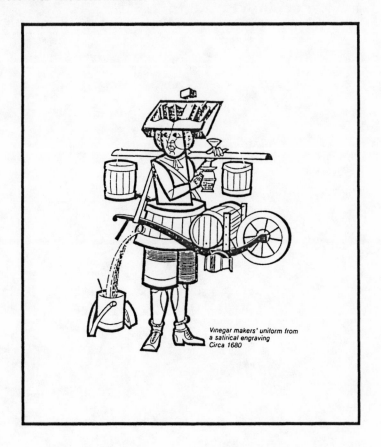

Vinegar makers' uniform from
a satirical engraving
Circa 1680

# CHAPTER 1

# VINEGAR "THE HISTORY"

&ast; &ast; &ast; &ast; &ast;

## CHAPTER 1
## CULTURAL HISTORY

Vinegar was a part of the human story even before we began writing down what we were doing. Since it is the natural result of the refining of alcoholic beverages, we can safely say that it has been around as long as beer, wine and other spirits. Some people erroneously refer to this as spoilage, but that is like saying that wine is spoiled grape juice

Like most other important discoveries, it was probably the result of an accident. "Someone left the wine out in the air.' But the earliest known recordings of vinegar find it already in common and varied use, so we have no idea how it was discovered. It was also discovered by many different cultures independently, so we have no real proof of where it was first discovered or how it spread to every corner of the globe.

Like beer, wine and other fermented foods, the ancients explained vinegar production differently than we do today. Like most other things, they believed, or said they believed, it was the result of some actions by the gods. And who can say that they were altogether wrong or that current theories are entirely correct. We have no evidence that they had a means of being aware of micro-organisms, so we feel safe in assuming that they did not know of acetobacters, the organisms responsible for the production of vinegar. But like scientist today, these fellows rarely told all they knew. And when they did speak, they most often spoke in code or riddles, so we don't really know what they knew.

We do know that they made and used beer and wine. Since wine and beer have been in the diet of mankind for roughly 10,000 years, it is assumed that vinegar has also been around for about that long.

## BABYLONIANS

One of the earliest recordings of vinegar was made by the Babylonians in about 5000 BC.[1] The Babylonians were noted at that time for the cultivation of date trees. And it was from these fine dates that they first made their prized vinegar. Each tree produced about 360 liters of dates. These were used primarily for making date wine and date vinegar.

Vinegar was made from the date fruit as well as the rest of the tree. The dates contained quite a bit of sugar. In fact, a kind of date honey was also made from the dates. The sugar from the dates could be turned into alcohol and then to vinegar.

Materials covering the tree stems also contained sugar. It is not clear how the Babylonians extracted the sugar from the date palm tree, but some people have suggested that it was done in much the same way it is done in Saudi Arabia today. There they tap the trees when they are in full blossom. The sap they retrieve is about as sweet as grape juice. This juice will quite readily turn into palm wine. And since its alcohol content is suitable for the growth of vinegar-producing bacteria, it must be drunk right away or it will sour. If Babylonians wanted to keep it longer, they had to add date honey to the palm juice. This additional sugar would raise the alcohol level and thus preserve the wine longer. In fact, the "state schnapps" was said to be so strong that it was not likely to turn into vinegar unless it was watered down.

Vinegar was also be made from beer. The residuals from beer making were mixed with water to make a "thin" beer, which was then allowed to turn into vinegar.

There was a saying in Babylonia that "beer that went sour wandered into the kitchen." For a while, it was quite common for people to make different kinds of alcohol in their homes. When these homemade products went sour, it seems that the clever Babylonians found uses for them in the kitchen. And it appears from the records left behind that this sour beer was a very common cooking item.

By 3000 BC, the making of homemade vinegar seems to have been phased out. The homemade variety had given way to a commercial industry that seems to have reached a rather large size by the year 2000 BC.

This industry was apparently part of a very large brewing industry, which was keenly aware of the relationship between alcohol and vinegar. It even assigned special people to watch the beer and wine to avoid the conditions that turned these drinks into vinegar. The residuals from the making of alcoholic beverages were used for soft drinks as well as vinegar. The dates and grains were soaked with water and pressed again to make these other products. These new products resulted in the creation of whole new businesses.

The Babylonians must also be given the credit for discovering many of the uses for vinegar. One of their most interesting inovations was the addition of herbs and spices to alter the taste and aroma of vinegar and anything to which the vinegar was added. They used tarragon, ruda, lavender, celery, mint, abysenth, portulaca and saffron.[2] In addition to improving the taste and aroma, these herbs and spices also increased the preservative effect of the vinegar when it was used for pickling.[3]

## ASSYRIANS

The Assyrians prescribed vinegar as a topical application for ear problems in their medical text. This treatment is still the treatment of choice for many chronic middle-ear diseases.[4] (See medical uses for more on this.)

# EGYPTIANS

The early Egyptians left no known written record of vinegar.[5] This is particularly interesting. They talked about their wines turning sour and the beer they made should have turned easily into vinegar, so it is inconceivable the Egyptians were ignorant of vinegar. Yet none of the early religious, historical, secular or medical text seem to mention the word vinegar. The most plausible explanation for this is that it is one of the Egyptian hieroglyphic words which have not be translated .

When we do find the word vinegar appearing in Egyptian writings, it appears as a foreign word.(see chapter 13) After the Greeks invaded Egypt, it is mentioned by Pliny. This well-known Roman naturalist and historian told about whole volumes that had been written on how to keep wine from turning sour. He mentioned also that an excellent quality of vinegar was made from the Cyprus fig and that an even better quality came from Alexandria.[6].

There is also a rather well-known and colorful story of the famous black Egyptian queen, Cleopatra, and Mark Antony. This rather clever African woman won a large wager with Mark Antony by using vinegar in a unique way.

Mark Antony had gone out of his way to impress the great queen and had spent a large sum of money on various feasts in doing so. But one day Cleopatra complained and mocked his efforts. Mark Antony was a bit upset and demanded to know how anyone could do more or spend more on a meal than he had done. She replied that she would prepare a meal that would cost 10 million sestertii. Antony, thinking that it was impossible to for a meal to cost that much, made a wager with Cleopatra that she couldn't do it.

After a couple of days, the wagered feast was prepared and though it was a great and royal feast there was nothing to even suggest a price tag of 10 million sestertii.

Seeing this, Mark Antony laughed at her and in a mocking way demanded to see the bill to account for the expense of the meal. To this Cleopatra replied that what they had already consumed was in addition to the wagered sum. She added that she would now consume her portion of the meal, which would cost 60 million sestertii. She then summoned the waiters to bring in a cruet of strong vinegar.

She was adorned with two of the most prized pearls known at that time. These pearls reputedly had come to her from great kings of the East by way of inheritance.

As Mark Antony watched, wondering what she was going to do, she removed one of the pearls, placed it in the vinegar and when it had dissolved, she drank it.

She was just about to prepare the same drink for him when Plancus, the judge of the wager, stopped her and declared that Cleopatra had won the bet. Mark Antony fell into a fit of anger.

Following this episode, Cleopatra was taken prisoner and all of her estate confiscated. The other pearl was cut in two and hung on the ears of a statue of Venus in Rome in the temple of Pantheon.[7]

Some authorities believe that Pliny's account of this tale is less than accurate. They say that vinegar cannot dissolve pearl and that she merely swallowed the pearl and recovered it later. In order to investigate the plausibility of this story, the author dissolved pearls in food-strength vinegar.

These photos show the effects of vinegar on pearls. This pearl (left) was dissolved in 10 percent acetic acid which would be considered the strongest vinegar possible with their technology. Note the bubbles in the chemical reaction (center). All that is left is the plastic "seed" of the cultured pearl. (right).

Since we do not know what strength of vinegar was used and under what circumstances it was used, we cannot say for sure what she did. But whatever she did, she used vinegar to prepare one of the most expensive meals in history. This episode also points out that the Egyptians had a rather thorough knowledge of vinegar.

Dioscorides traveled through Egypt with Nero's army. His writings documented many Egyptian medicines in which vinegar or vinegar combined with honey, brine, thyme or squill was used for many different illnesses.

The Egyptians also used vinegar for mushroom poisoning, worms in the ears, bleeding wounds, severe loss of appetitite and gangrene, among other things.[8]

# JEWS

Another reason we know that the Egyptians must have been familiar with vinegar is that the Jews were intimate with vinegar and refer to it often in their literature. And, of course, the Jews and the Egyptians share quite a bit of history.

Since early Jewish literature makes a distinction between "vinegar of wine," homez yayin and "vinegar of strong drink," homez shekar,[9] it is certain that vinegar was a very familiar item. It was apparently quite common to produce vinegar from palm wine and cider, but the people of that time and region must have known of many substances from which to make vinegar.

It was used to wet the flat loaves of bread that were commonly eaten at that time. It was mixed with water and used as a drink, though it couldn't cure thirst by itself. Pickles and meat were preserved in vinegar. Lettuce and endives were dipped into it. It was used as a condiment. Vinegar was also useful in freeing olives from their pits.

Aside from culinary uses, vinegar served as an astringent as well as an agent for soothing and cooling the body. In fact, because of this calming effect, vinegar is forbidden on the day of atonement. It was employed for combatting dandruff, used as a gargle for toothache and even as a dressing for wounds. It was also used a a mordant for dying.[10]

In those days, the price of vinegar was about the same as the price of wine. The prices were influenced by and fluctuated with one another. The Hakalah even discussed whether wine and vinegar should be considered the same thing.

The most familiar piece of Jewish literature, the Old Testament of the Bible, first mentions vinegar in the Book of Numbers, the 6th chapter and third verse. It is here that the God of the Jews commanded that when either a man or woman separated themselves to vow a vow of a Nazarite, to separate themselves unto the Lord, he or she should do certain things. On top of the list was the commandment that "he shall separate himself from wine and strong drink, and shall drink, no vinegar of wine or vinegar of strong drink, neither shall he drink any liquor of grapes nor moist grapes, or dried."

Jewish wine, which is intended for the altar is not supposed to be fermented and has to be levitically clean. It is not clear how they met these requirements, since vinegar is a product of double or triple fermentation. Today, we know of ways to make acetic acid without fermentation, but we have no conclusive evidence that they knew of these same methods then.

The Hakalah forbade the use of vinegar of the Gentiles since it was prepared with forbidden wine. The question was even raised as to whether wine that had turned to vinegar should be prohibited if even touched by a Gentile .

It is interesting to note that the passage in the Book of Numbers refers to drinking vinegar. It apparently was a practice even then to use vinegar as a beverage, a practice which still exists today with many people. However, Psalms 69, the 21st verse, "They gave me gall for my meat and in my thirst they gave me vinegar to drink," makes it difficult to discern what place vinegar held as a drink.

One possible explanation is that diluted vinegar is a rather pleasant drink and sweetened a bit is actually quite delicious. On the other hand, straight vinegar, at say 5 percent or 6 percent, is practically impossible to drink.

Vinegar appears again in the Bible in the Book of Ruth, the second chapter and the 14th verse: "And Boaz said unto her, 'At meal time come hither, and eat of the bread, and dip thy morsel in the vinegar...."

From this verse we can see that it was a practice to dip morsels of bread into vinegar as a kind of sauce. This was a practice that the Jews apparently shared with other people of that time and region.

Proverbs, the 10th verse and 26th chapter points out that "as vinegar to the teeth, and as smoke to the eyes, so is the sluggard to them that send him."

The book of Proverbs the 25th chapter  and the 20th verse reads, "As he that taketh away a garment in cold weather, and as vinegar upon nitre (bicarbonate of soda), so is he that singeth songs to a heavy heart."

These verses illustrate that the Jews knew of the chemical reactions of vinegar on various things. And since it is used in a figurative sense, these reactions must have been common knowledge. This serves as further proof that Jews have long been quite knowledgeable about vinegar.

In the New Testament, we find four references to vinegar, but they are all related to the same story as told by four different men, Mathew, Mark, Luke and John. When Jesus was crucified, we find these four accounts of his  encounter with vinegar in his last moments as a man on earth.

St. Mathew 27, verse 37, "They gave him vinegar to drink mingled with gall: and when he had tasted thereof , he would not drink."

St. Mathew 27, verse 48 "And straight away one of them ran , and took a sponge, and filled it with vinegar, and put it on a reed, and gave it him to drink."

St. Mark 16, verse 36,"And one ran and filled a sponge full of vinegar, and put it on a reed, and gave him to drink, saying let alone; let us see whether Elias will come to take him down.

St. Luke 23, verse 36, "And the soldiers also mocked him, coming to him, and offering him vinegar."

St. John 20, verse 29 ; "Now there was set a vessel full of vinegar : and they filled a sponge with vinegar, and put it upon hysop, and put it to his mouth."

St. John 20, verse 30; "When Jesus therefore had received the vinegar, he said, "it is finished" bowed his head, and gave up the ghost."

Notice that each of the four writers give a slightly different account of the events, though they are substantially the same. The drink referred to in St. Mathew 27, verse. 37 was probably intended as a narcotic. We draw this conclusion from the fact that the word gall in Hebrew translates through the Greek to opium. It appears that this concoction was commonly given to people about to be executed. [11]

It is important to realize that the drink that Jesus was given was most probably *posca,* a diluted vinegar that was the common and popular drink of the poorer classes and the Roman soldiers. It was very common for the soldiers to keep this drink with them at all times. (See Roman use of vinegar.) The final offering of vinegar to Jesus was in his response to his declaration that he was thirsty. So it appears that the offering of vinegar was quite likely a benevolent act by Roman soldiers whose government had agreed to crucify Jesus as a political concession to the Jewish leaders.

One writer, Rosenmuller, conjectures that it may have been given as a stimulant to keep the victim alive during the torture, but this seems to be a minority opinion. [12]

What we can see without conjecture is that the last request Jesus made was filled with vinegar. And the last thing Jesus had to drink before leaving the world as a man was vinegar!

## GREEKS

The Greeks also had many uses for vinegar. One of the most valued was that of making pickles. They mixed various assortments of herbs, flowers, roots and vegetables and preserved them in vinegar. They stored these delicacies in wide-mouthed cylindrical jars for extended periods. The recipes for these were executed with the greatest of care. The plants were often macerated and then impregnated, drop by drop, with various solutions of vinegar, oil and salt. They also cut meat into small pieces and treated it in the same manner.[13]

The famous Spartan soldiers liked to eat a black broth reputedly made of vinegar, pork stock and salt.[14]

But the most famous of the Greeks to use vinegar extensively was Hippocrates. From the writings of "the father of modern medicine," we find that he prescribed it for all kinds of ailments. This will be discussed more thoroughly in the section on the medical uses of vinegar.

Another famous Greek, Theophrastus, mixed vinegar with pepper to make a potion for reviving a victim of suffocation.[15]

It is clear from these references that the Greeks were very familiar with vinegar and that it occupied an important place in many facets of their lives.

## ROMANS

Vinegar occupied a special place in Roman lives. Pliny, the well known naturalist and historian, declared that in vinegar "there are considerable virtues and without which we should miss many of the comforts of civilized life."[16] He cited the Cyprian fig as being particularly good for making a high-quality vinegar. He also pointed out that vinegar from Alexandria was of exceptional quality.[17]

The Romans used vinegar extensively in their cooking and at their meals.[18] It was used as a dip for various foods. They often sweetened it to improve the taste.[19] Diluted, it was referred to as posca, the poor mans' wine, and was quite popular with the common people and the Roman soldiers. The Roman soldiers kept the vinegar full strength and diluted it whenever they wanted a drink. Pescennius of Niger restricted his troops from drinking anything but posca!

The sailors around Pliny's time used vinegar to calm the seas of typhoons. They apparently threw vinegar out at the waves as the waves approached a ship during a storm. They also thought that vinegar was good for putting out fires, since it had the reputation of having a cold nature.[20]

## HANNIBAL, THE GREAT AFRICAN GENERAL

One of the greatest generals the world has ever known was Hannibal. And of all of the stories told about this famous African, his crossing of the Alps with his army on elephants is the most colorful and enduring. Most of what we know about this march comes to us from the writings of Titus Livius, a famous historian who lived around the time of Christ.

In order to move his army, mounted on elephants, over the Alps it was necessary to cut a new path through these rugged mountains. When he came upon huge boulders that blocked his path, he used a bit of chemistry to solve the problem. He had his men heat the stones with an intense fire and then pour vinegar on them. This action literally turned the stone into powder. After removing the remaining debris, he was then able to strike terror into the Roman empire.[21]

## CHINA

We can find vinegar used as a food preservative in China from from very ancient times. Text written during the Chou period (1122 B.C. - 256 B.C.) mentions *liu* as a seasoning. It is generally thought that this word translates as vinegar, but we have no information about how or of what it was made.

### Han
### (202 BC-220 AD)

During the Han period, vinegar was almost always included in any major feast as a seasoning.[22]

### Ch'in
### 221 BC-206 BC

During the Ch'in era, meat was served that was flavored by pressing crushed garlic and salt into it and then soaking it with wine vinegar.[23]

### Tang
### (618-906 AD).

We find vinegar in common use during the Tang dynasty It was made from a variety of materials, including grape juice, peaches, wheat and rice. The flavor of their vinegars was sometimes enhanced by the addition of kumquat leaves from southern China. They were even reported to have used peach blossoms to change the flavor of vinegar.[24] The use of such a wide variety of substances to make vinegar implies a thorough knowledge of the art of making vinegar.

Meat pickles, called *hai* were a very important class of pickled products. The name *shih* was also given to preparations that included vinegar. Among the articles pickled by the Chinese were: fish and meats of various kinds, including deer, rabbit, goat and sheep. These pickles were the pickles of royalty. Crabs preserved in vinegar were a favorite in the Imperial Court.

Venison preserved with ginger and vinegar was prized as a delicious food as well as a tonic. The Chinese used the sika deer, the musk deer, the water deer, the tufted deer and the muntjac for these pickles.

In the south of China, a popular soup was made from the flesh and bones of goats, deer, chicken and pigs and enriched with various combinations of herbs, spices and vinegar. [25]

## Sung
## (960-1279 AD)

During the Sung dynasty, vinegar was also very important. Wu Tzu-Mu recorded that "the things that people cannot do without every day are firewood, rice, oil, salt, soybean sauce, tea and vinegar. Though they be the poorest people, this must always be so." The seven necessities, as this list came to be known, provided the carbohydrates from the rice, the proteins from the soybeans and the the various vitamins and minerals from the vinegar preparations.

The Chinese even used vinegar substitutes. A common one during the Tang and Sung dynasties was a juice extracted from the bark of the yuan tree. The exact identity of this tree is unknown, but it is said to resemble the chestnut tree. The juice of this tree was used in the preservation of duck eggs. The eggs turned a characteristic brown when pickled in this liquid. [26]

## Yüan and Ming
## (1279-1644 AD)

The importance of vinegar during the Yüan (1279-1368) dynasty is underscored by a line in a drama. A busy housewife declares that "from the moment I get up in the morning, I am busy about the seven things, fuel, rice, oil, salt, soy sauce, vinegar and tea." [27]

The Ming Dynasty (1368-1644 AD) stipulated in the Ancestral Admonitions (Huang Ming tsu-hsün-lu) that among the various and separate bureaus designated to taking care of the needs of the Imperial Court, an imperial vinegar works be set up. Specially trained palace eunics were responsible for the production and quality of the vinegar. [28]

During this period, vinegar was described as acidly sweet and bitter with a slightly warm character. The bitterness in vinegar is now believed to be caused by the infection of the vinegar with undesirable organisms. But it could have been from bitter rice beer (aka rice wine). It is not known whether the bitterness in Chinese vinegar was by accident or design. We do know that the Chinese ideogram for vinegar indicates that bitterness was closely associated with vinegar.

In this period vinegar was thought to counteract the poisons in the flesh of fish, melons and vegetables. Rice vinegar was especially prized. But Chia Ming, a scholar and food writer during that period, thought that too much of it would damage the flesh, bones and stomach. He also warned people who were suffering from colds, diarrhea or malaria or who were taking medicine to avoid vinegar. It is important to note however, that Chia Mings medical advice was not shared by Chinese physicians. And it was pointed out by Chinese scholars that to observe all of the warnings and taboos cited by him would make eating virtually impossible (see Chinese medicinal uses of vinegar- chapter 11).

## Ch'ing
## (Manchu  1644-1912)

Even as late as the Ch'ing dynasty, vinegar was considered one of the staples in the Chinese diet. Yüan Mei was one of the most important scholars during the Ch'ing period. He studied and wrote prolifically about food during his time. He advised that one should guard against vinegar which was finely colored and/or weakly acetic. Chen-chiang vinegar was said to suffer from these flaws. The best vinegar was thought to be from Pan-p'u in Kiangsu. The second-best was from P'u-k'ou in Chekiang.

Another important food writer was Li Yü. During his time, Li was criticized for the austerity of his recipes, but he did occasionally come up with some reasonably exotic ones. One called for a small amount of vinegar to flavor a broth that would be poured over noodles that had been prepared with sesame and bamboo shoots and flavored with a sauce of mushrooms or shrimp.

## Modern China

In modern China, vinegar is still used extensively. We find it in everything from vinegared rice to thinly sliced jellyfish skin in a vinegar sauce.

Chinese food can be broadly divided between Northern and Southern Chinese cuisine. Northern Chinese cooking uses considerably less vinegar than southern Chinese cooking. But there are exceptions to this rule. The Shansi province, for example, is famous for its vinegar. Visitors to T'ai-yüan, the capitol of this province, have commented that the cooks there could not even poach an egg without the addition of vinegar.

Southern Chinese cuisine on the other hand, uses vinegar quite extensively. On the table of almost any Cantonese restaurant can almost always be found a peppered oil and a cruet of vinegar. Hundreds of dips for the many Cantonese delicacies include vinegar as a base. Its profuse use in Southern China is one of the major distinctions that separates Southern from Northern Chinese cooking. [29]

# JAPAN

Though it is quite probable that the Japanese knew how to make and use vinegar much earlier, the first time we find documentation of vinegar in Japanese historical writings is in the early imperial archives. It was during the reign of Emperor Ojin, about 399-404 A.D., that vinegar-making techniques crossed the Japan Sea along with rice wine making from China.[30]

During this period, Osaka was the center of culture in Japan, and so it is here that we find vinegar making refined. More specifically, it was in the Izumi section of Osaka prefecture. As a result, the old records will refer to vinegar as either Izumi vinegar or bitter sake.

In 645 AD. a centralized government was formed and new national laws were established. Under these laws the government created eight positions that were assigned the task of overseeing the making of food and beverages. One of these positions was called the "Miki no Tsukas." The holder of that title was responsible for overseeing the making of vinegar in addition to sake and other alcoholic beverages.

In the "Manyo-shu," a collection of songs, poems and other literary documents written in the Nara era, there is a recipe for a dish that includes different condiments combined with vinegar. It seems from these and other writings that the Japanese were as familiar with pickled deer meat as the Chinese were.

## Heian period
## (794-1192)

But it was not until the Heian period that we find documentation that vinegar had been developed into an art form. By this time, the Japanese were using plum vinegar, iris vinegar and miscellaneous fruit vinegars, as well as rice and sake vinegars.

They distinguished rice vinegar from sake vinegar even though the origin of the vinegars were the same. Rice vinegar was made directly from rice while sake vinegar was made by adding rice vinegar to sake.

They also made a vinegar called Mannen-su, which means 10,000-year vinegar or eternal vinegar. This vinegar was made by taking vinegar out of a mixture from which it was made and adding an equal part of sake and water that was then acidified into vinegar.

Iris vinegar was made by adding iris leaves to a mixture of water, aged sake and vinegar.

## Muromachi period
## (1400-1603)

During the Muromachi period, vinegar gained wide acceptance as a spice for cooking in Japan. Condiments such as vinegar-miso, ginger vinegar-miso, sansho vinegar-miso, wasabi (a kind of horse radish) vinegar and walnut vinegar became popular.

## Edo period
## (1603-1868)

During the Edo period, mass production of vinegar was
established.

**VINEGAR COMMERCE IN JAPAN**

## Meiji period
## (1868  1912)

**VINEGAR COMMERCE IN JAPAN**

During the Meiji period, the Japanese began to create new products, using foreign food-processing techniques. During this period, the best of these products were given imperial palace designation. This honor marked a product that was deemed fit for the emperor, who was believed to be a descendant of the gods. Nakano Matazaemon, known today as Mitsukan-su, received that honor for vinegar in 1900 (Meiji 33). This practice was continued until 1948.

## Modern Japan

Today Japan is among the world leaders in research and development as well as production of vinegar. And some of the finest vinegars in the world are made there. Here, as in most other modern countries, vinegar plays a key role in the health, nutritional and industrial welfare of the country.

# EUROPE
# FROM 17TH CENTURY

The Europeans from the Middle Ages until modern times have always had a use for vinegar. We are most familiar with its use in cooking. In 1375, one of the first known cookbooks of post-Roman Europe, "Viandier de Taillevent", was written by Guillaume Tirel, the personal chef of Charles V of France. In this prized work Tirel gave a recipe for camiline that called for mixing ginger, cloves, cinnamon, cardamom, mace and long pepper, then squeezing out bread soaked in. vinegar, straining out all of this together and salting to taste. [31]

When Europeans were expanding their world, one of the problems they encountered was the lack of food during the long sailing voyages. One of the common foods was a kind of biscuit. This was a simple mixture of flour and water that was baked and dried until it was so hard that it was nearly impossible to break, even by hand. In order to eat the biscuits, the sailors soaked them in their water rations until they became porridge-like. They then improved the taste of this porridge by adding vinegar and a bit of salt pork. This combination of vinegar and salt pork gave a kind of dignity to dishes like Lobscouse, Scotch coffee and Skillygolee. [32]

During the 17th century in Britain, when the cities smelled offensive, people would use sponges soaked in vinegar to deodorize their immediate surroundings. They often carried these sponges in small silver boxes. The Victorian ladies, who

were known for their "vapors," restored themselves with
vinegar soaked-cloths, which they placed across their foreheads.

There was a time when vinegar cakes were very popular. At that
time vinegar took the place of eggs.[33] The inclusion of vinegar
into British food preparation techniques made it possible to
transport food over longer distances without it spoiling. This
meant that people in the inland area could enjoy seafood on a
more regular basis. [34]

The great sea power for which the British were famous was
made possible in part by vinegar. Mark Beaufoy built a healthy
business with contracts to supply vinegar to the British navy.
The vinegar was not only used to preserve food for the long sea
journeys, it was also used as a detergent to clean the decks of
the ships.

MAKING VINEGAR IN BRITAIN

The famous French chef La Varenne recommended a sauce that was basically meat drippings and vinegar. This sauce is still an expensive luxury in France. [35]

During the reign of Louis XIII, the Duc de la Meilleraye, the grand master of the artillery of France, presented the french government with a bill of 1,300,000 francs for vinegar that was used to cool the cannons. The bill was paid without protest.[36]

The great wines of France have produced some of the finest vinegars ever made. The process of making some of the finest vinegars possible is named after the French town of Orleans, which is legendary for its fine vinegars.

## WESTERN MEDICAL HISTORY

Europeans also used vinegar for medicinal purposes. They had formulas for antiseptic vinegars, ascorbic vinegars, camphorated vinegars, colchicum vinegars, quill vinegar, black drop vinegar and syrup of vinegar.

There was also a famous vinegar known as the "Vinegar of the Four Thieves." During the great plague in Europe, some people made their living by liberating the belongings of the departed. Some of these thieves, despite their constant contact with the disease, were never stricken. It was believed that their immunity came from a vinegar based medicine that became known as the "Vinegar of the four theives.[37] (see chapter 11)

## VINEGAR IN AMERICAN HISTORY

Vinegar was used among the soldiers of the American Civil War to prevent scurvy. [38] Its use as an antibiotic has been known and appreciated since Biblical times, and vinegar was used during World War I to treat wounds.

We mentioned earlier that the Assyrians used vinegar for ear diseases. In "modern" American medical practice, it is used for acute external otitis, a serious ear infection.[39]

Dr. D.C. Jarvis, a famous proponent of vinegar for medicinal uses, offers many uses for apple cider vinegar. Apple cider vinegar is used to make applications to treat many diseases, including lameness, burns, night sweats, poison ivy, shingles, varicose veins, ringworm and impetigo.[40]

According to The Pharmacological Basis of Therapeutics, a modern medical text, vinegar is still used in a wide variety of medical applications. Physicians use it for surgical dressings and bladder irrigations as well as the treatment of burns and infections (see chapter 11 for more on this topic.).[41]

# CHAPTER 2

## THE LEGAL HISTORY OF VINEGAR

In nature, alcohol and vinegar fermentation happens almost simultaneously. As soon as the wild yeast start to turn the fallen vegetation into alcohol, acid-forming bacteria attack the alcohol and produce what we have long called vinegar. It is difficult to say how many years ago man learned to take advantage of this natural process, but a good guess is that he learned that vinegar was a product of alcohol fermentation early in the game because of the relationship between the alcohol and vinegar-producing organisms.

### WHAT IS VINEGAR?

Today, it is agreed that vinegar is essentially acetic acid, but acetic acid is not vinegar. However, this has not always been the case. Because acetic acid can be made in a number of different and cheaper ways than vinegar, there have been, and continues to be, attempts to pass it off to consumers as vinegar.

Those who make real vinegar do so at considerably more expense and trouble than those who make the imitation article. The manufacturers of good vinegar are put to a serious disadvantage when they have to compete with those products made from petroleum or other fusel oils.

The consumer suffers most from these fake vinegars. When the consumer is made aware of the differences, they almost always prefer true vinegar to the bogus.

It took a lot of scientific study and legal debate to finally settle the question of what exactly constitutes vinegar vs. acetic acid and how to let the consumer know what he is buying.

Since this book will probably be most widely read in English-speaking countries and English law forms the base of the legal system in those countries, we will take a look at how the English courts settled this question.


## THE BRITISH PERSPECTIVE

The earliest known writings for specific methods of making vinegar were made in 50 AD by Columella.[42] In these volumes he gave all of the details for making three kinds of vinegar. He told how to make vinegar from grapes, figs and burnt barley. And though there are many classical records on how vinegar was used, records in English do not begin until the 14th century. This is probably because, after the Romans left Britain in about 410 AD, England was in an almost constant state of petty warfare until the Normans finally brought it under their rule.

After 1350, however, we find a number of manuscripts that talk about vinegar. Documents like "Forme of Curry" and "Ancient Cookery" list more than 480 recipes in which vinegar is used. [43] Many other references are listed in various 15th century cookbooks that can be found in British museums.

With the introduction of the printing press at the end of the 15th century, many cookbooks appeared. In 1500, "A Noble Booke Feastes Royal and of Cokerie" was published. Between 1500 and 1850, more than 300 cookbooks were written and published, and almost all of them gave instructions for making vinegar by alcohol and acetic fermentation. Hannah Whooley published "The Queenlike Closet" in 1669. She included recipes on how to make rose and cowslip vinegar. In 1747 Hannah Glasse wrote, "The Art of Cookery Made Plain and Easy" and introduced six different vinegars and gave instructions on how to make them. By 1850 "The New London Cookery" was introducing 30 different vinegars with instructions on how to make many of them. "Mrs. Beatons Household Management", published in 1860, also included lessons on the making of many different vinegars.

But by this time the Industrial Revolution was in full swing and the number of different kinds of vinegar that were made in the home rapidly declined. Industry started to make mass produced food for all of the factory workers who were too busy and tired to make it for themselves. With this change also came a decrease in the quality of taste and, worse, an increase in the adulteration of vinegar. This problem of adulteration has been the chief cause of the introduction of legislation and subsequent litigation concerning vinegar. [44]

Another important event that occurred around this time was the publication of the first modern scientific work on vinegar by Louis Pasteur. [45] Most of what we know about vinegar today has its roots in this work. There is also a strong connection between his findings and the findings of legal institutions on what exactly constitutes real vinegar. So it is quite probable that these scientific advances affected the findings of the courts.

The chief question about vinegar have been concerned with what actually constitutes real vinegar. The primary constituent of vinegar is acetic acid, but science and industry are able to make acetic acid by means other than fermentation. And since this product lacks many of the other important trace elements found in the naturally brewed product, can we say that the acetic acid is vinegar?

During the later half of the 1800's, commercial acetic acid was produced on a large scale, primarily from calcium acitate. The calcium acitate was obtained from the destructive distillation of wood. Acetic acid produced in this way was very pure, strong and comparatively cheap. It was known as glacial acetic acid and it was virtually 100 percent pure acetic acid.

It was necessary and therefore customary to reduce this concentration down to 4 percent -5 percent so that it would be similar to fermented vinegar. It was then colored with caramel or burnt sugar to improve its taste and appearance and sold in the market as vinegar. This "imitation " vinegar was often labeled as wood vinegar, pure vinegar or table vinegar.

In fermented vinegar, we find many chemicals not found in acetic acid. We also find many vitamins, particularly riboflavin, nicotinic acid, Vitamin B-1 and mineral salts. Very important to the taste of the vinegar is the inclusion of esters and higher alcohols.

By 1900, a report to the local government board in Great Britain stated that:"The mixture of acetic acid and water entirely lacks the aroma of a brewed vinegar. It has, however, certain characteristics in common with brewed vinegar in virtue of the acetic acid which both contain. But very generally an artificial vinegar possesses, in addition to its acidity, a harshness and pungency which seem inseparable from the use of acetic acid not made by process of fermentation."

The report went on to state that: "It appears to be in the interest of the consumer that vinegar which has been prepared by coloring and flavoring a solution of acetic acid should not be represented as merely vinegar or malt vinegar but should be sold under some designation which, if it retains the word vinegar, should also make the nature of the product apparent. Artificial vinegars, as a class, are inferior in taste and flavor to vinegars which are solely the product of alcoholic and acetous fermentation of saccharin liquors usually employed for the purpose."

In December of 1911, the local government issued a declaration that "vinegar is liquid derived wholly from alcoholic-acetous fermentation. It shall contain not less than 4 grams of acetic acid $CH_3COOH$ in 100 cubic centimeters of vinegar. Nor shall it contain any substance or coloring matter except caramel."

The board also decided that malt vinegar is vinegar which is wholly derived from malted barley or from cereals, the starch of which has been sacharified by diatase of malt.

The opinion of the local government board was accepted in principle by the society of public analysts, which added that if the word "vinegar" were used in connection with acetic acid, the prefix of "imitation" or "artificial ' must also be added so that the public would know exactly what it was getting.

However no legislative weight was given to these views. When a Private Members Bill was introduced in 1926 to give weight to such views, it was defeated.

In the meantime the trade in imitation vinegar continued to grow. Large quantities of this chemical were sold as vinegar, pure vinegar, table vinegar and even malt vinegar. But there were a few bright spots.

In the case of Preston vs. Jackson, 1928,[46] the high court ruled that the acetic acid as table vinegar violated the sale of food and drugs act. In 1930 the Westminster City Council summoned a shopkeeper for "selling table vinegar not of the nature and substance of the quality demanded." The chief magistrate at Bow street heard long testimony from many expert analysts and witnesses. After pondering the evidence he admonished: "Bearing in mind the fact that for some 300 years the substance sold as vinegar was the product of fermentation and it was admitted for the defence that it is produced in a way which undoubtedly gives a better aroma and flavor, I have come to the conclusion that it is not permissible to sell as vinegar or table vinegar a substance which is not the product of fermentation"

The defendant appealed in London sessions, and a great volume of evidence was presented on both sides. The Chief magistrate's decision was upheld, and the appeal dismissed the defendant fined 75 guineas.

As a result of this decision, the Association of Pure Vinegar Manufacturers, which had supported the appeal, decided to change its name to the Association of Non-Brewed Vinegar

Manufacturers. It then counseled its members to label their diluted acidic acid as non-brewed vinegar.

In 1945, a retailer was prosecuted under the Merchandise Marks Act for selling non-brewed vinegar that was labeled as such. This was on the grounds that he had falsely labeled his merchandise. For three days, the experts testified on both sides of the issue. The chief magistrate decided that non-brewed vinegar was, in fact, a false trade description.

In the 1949 case of Diment vs. Kat, Chief Magistrate Sir Lawrence Dunn concluded that: "Vinegar has been well-known in this country since medieval times and it was, until the year 1840 or 1850, invariably the result of double fermentation, alcoholic and acetous. About that time, there was discovered a method of making synthetic acid by destructive distillation of wood. This pyroligneous acid or, as it subsequently came to be called, wood vinegar, did not come into general use as a condiment certainly before 1850, and not seriously until 1890. The fermented liquor may be obtained from malt, wine , cider or spirits. In each case, the first fermentation consists in changing the sugar content of the liquid into alcohol. A second fermentation is then induced in which an organism, mycoderma aceta, produces further changes. In addition to producing acetic acid, it produces a number of secondary products called enzymes. These enzymes are responsible for the chief difference between the brewed and non-brewed product. The evidence has, I think, established that these secondary products confer on brewed vinegar a smoothness, bouquet and aroma superior to that of non-brewed liquor."

The chief magistrate further stated: "I was satisfied on the evidence called before me that vinegar can alone consist of a product of double fermentation as herein before described. And that the liquor sold as non-brewed vinegar was not vinegar. I was of the opinion that the term non-brewed vinegar consisted of vinegar as the genus and non-brewed as the species and that, consequently, the appellant's product, not being vinegar, and vinegar therefore being a false description thereof, non-brewed vinegar must be a false trade description."

The magistrate's decision was affirmed and the defendants appeal dismissed with a fine.[47]

After this set back the Association of Non-Brewed Manufacturers changed its name again. This time they became the Association of Non-Brewed Condiment Manufactures and announced that their product would now be called non-brewed condiment. It was then sold in some small general stores and markets selling vegetable and fish.[48]

## UNITED STATES LEGAL HISTORY

In the United States the first legal definition of vinegar came under the Federal Food and Drugs Act of 1906. It was later revised in a service and regulatory announcement in 1933. Under this act six types of vinegar are defined (see vinegar composition index).

Under those guidelines the unqualified term vinegar could only be used in the United States to designate cider or apple cider vinegar. For many years cider vinegar was the only kind of vinegar that was sold in the United States, so it was thought that it was proper to consider that when consumers asked for vinegar they usually meant apple cider vinegar unless they specified otherwise. Also, even though vinegar can be made by a number of other materials, only six types are outlined under those federal guidelines.

Note also that acetic acid is not defined as vinegar.

## INTERNATIONAL STANDARDS

The World Health Organization of the United Nations has adopted the Spanish definition of vinegar as its standard in its "codex alimentarus."

*Vinegar has to be limpid with a characteristic flavor and color, without sediments or other perceptible alterations.*

*Vinegar should contain the characteristic substances according to its origin which have not been transformed as a result of its production.*

*The total acidity calculated as acetic acid anhydride should not be less than 50 grams per liter. (these range fro 3 percent to 6.percent in other countries)The dry extracts without sugars should be not less than 10 grams per liter.Total ash content should be less than one gram per liter. The total alcohol content should not be more than 1 percent.The total residue of sulphur dioxide should not be more than 50 milligrams per kilogram.*

Brazil and Italy forbid the use of synthetic acetic acid. Many other countries do not find the use of acetic acid very popular, even when it is not forbidden by law.

From a review of the legal, scientific, cultural and historical documents available, it appears that the universally accepted definition of vinegar is a product that is made by natural fermentation.

# CHAPTER 3

# THE PRODUCTION HISTORY

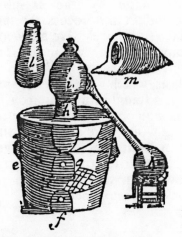

*e.*   A portable furnace for distilling
      with a fire of sand.
*f.*   The ash-room and its door.
*g.*   ,,   hearth and its door.
*h.*   ,,   cucurbit.
*i.*   ,,   head.
*k.*   ,,   receiver.
*l.*   ,,   cucurbit apart.
*m.*   ,,   head apart.

Early Apparatus for Distilling Vinegar.

As mentioned earlier, vinegar has been in production for quite a long time. However, the early practitioners of the art of making vinegar left no indications that they understood the living nature of vinegar. The earliest writings on the "mother of vinegar," the biological mat that covers vinegar made in the traditional way, were made by H. Booerhave in 1732. However, though it was mentioned, the contents of this mother of vinegar were not described or identified. This pelicule formation that appeared on vinegar was called mycoderma in 1822 by C.H. Persoon, but its biological nature was still not discussed.[49]

By 1837, however, the microbiological basis for vinegar production was realized[50] (see production for more biological history). In 1864, Louis Pasteur went on to confirm these findings in his "Memoirs sur la Fermentation Acetic."[51] He also wrote about other important findings in his book "Etudes sur le Vinaigre" published in 1858 in Paris. This was probably the first book to be written solely on the biological nature of vinegar.

Until relatively recently, vinegar was made by the let-alone method. In this process, the sugar in the fruit juices were allowed to convert into alcohol. This conversion was facilitated by yeasts, which were generally wild yeasts found in the nature. After this conversion had taken place, these wines were allowed to sit in open containers, which were partially filled to allow the free flow of air until this wine was converted into vinegar.

Filter over top of barrel.

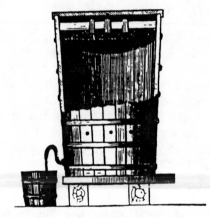

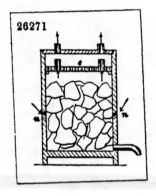

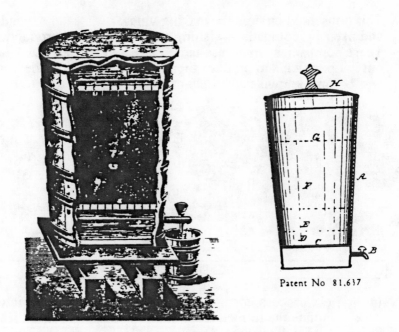

Patent No 81,637

OTHER DESIGNS FOR HOUSEHOLD PRODUCTION

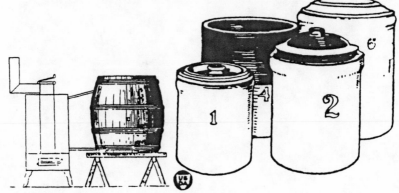

This household process for making vinegar was later expanded and used by companies wishing to increase their production. These companies would use large barrels of various sizes, laid out in open fields to produce their vinegar. This expanded process became known as the field process.

FIELD PROCESS

In the field process, a small amount of vinegar was put into a cask to initiate the fermentation of a previously produced fruit-based alcohol like wine. It was, no doubt, very difficult to control the quality of the vinegars made in this manner, but this was the process of choice for several hundred years. The so-called vinegar yard of Castle Street in Southward, England, was probably producing alegar in 1641, using the field process.[52]

## FIELD PROCESS

Some countries, notably England and Egypt, consumed more beer than wine. It is understandable, then, that their vinegar would be obtained from the souring of beer rather than wine. And just as vinegar meant sour wine, these products were known as alegars, since they were produced from the souring of ale or beer.

The first complete and detailed description of vinegar production was by Olivier de Serrres in 1616. [53] The Orleans method, named after the French city, is the oldest-known commercial method. This is still the process of choice for making a superior vinegar. It is also known as the slow process.

The Orleans system is actually a modification of the old field process (see Production Methods section for complete information on all of the systems discussed here).

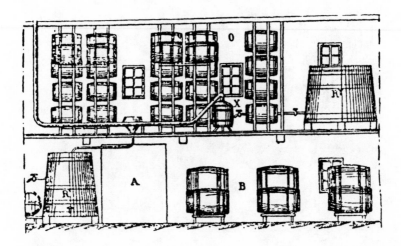

## FLOOR PLAN OF ORLEANS SYSTEM OF VINEGAR MAKING

This Orleans method is slow, usually taking from one to three months. It often takes even longer depending on the temperature and other factors. The efficiency of the fermentation was from 77 percent to 84 percent.

ORLEANS METHOD

One of the major problems with this method was the accumulation of the mother of vinegar, which generally filled up the barrel and slowed down production considerably. The manufacturers tried many ways to improve this method. One of the most notable improvements came from Louis Pasteur in 1868. He installed a wooden raft to hold up the mother of vinegar to keep it from sinking to the bottom of the barrel. But the method was basically the same one described in 1616 by Oiivier de Serrres.

## THE VINEGAR GENERATOR

The first significant change came from H. Boerhaave, the Dutch technologist who is credited with making the first vinegar generator. This device used various packing materials and a trickling principle.[54] This was the first major change in vinegar since the household method.

Boerhaave employed pomice as well as branches from various plants for packing materials. By using a device to drip the vinegar over the packing, the surface area of the liquid could be significantly increased. The increased surface makes more oxygen available to the vinegar producing bacteria and thereby increasing production.

Efforts to improve on the Boerhaave method resulted in what became known as the quick vinegar process. There is a lot of debate as to who deserves the credit for developing this method. Some people give the credit to Schutzenbach, others give it to Kastner. Still others give the credit to Boerhaave as the major contributor to the quick vinegar process. Schutzenbach is usually given the honor of inventing the "German Process"

During the 1800's and the early 1900's, many different patents were issued. The quantity of these patents indicated the interest and activity around vinegar at that time (see illustrations).

## VARIOUS DESIGNS OF VINEGAR PATENTS

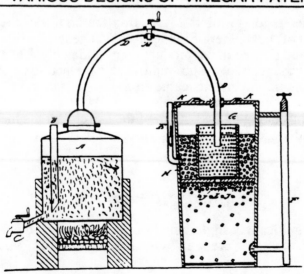

Patent No. 63,256,

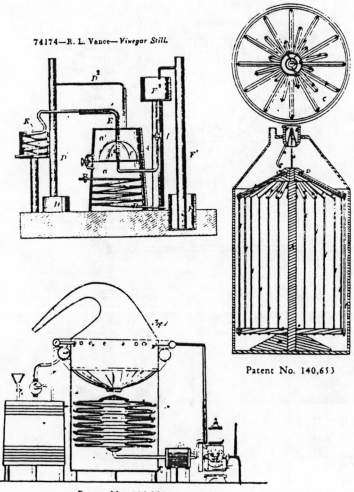

74174—R. L. Vance—*Vinegar Still.*

Patent No. 140,653

Patent No. 105,390

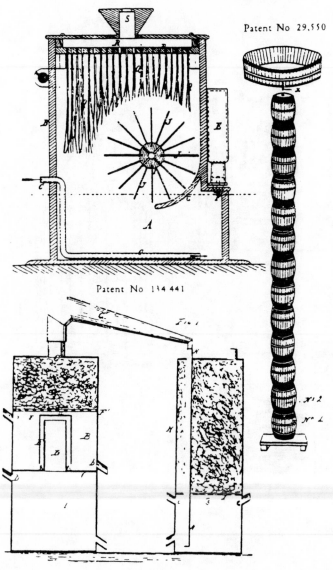

Patent No 29,550

Patent No 134 441

Patent No 93,012

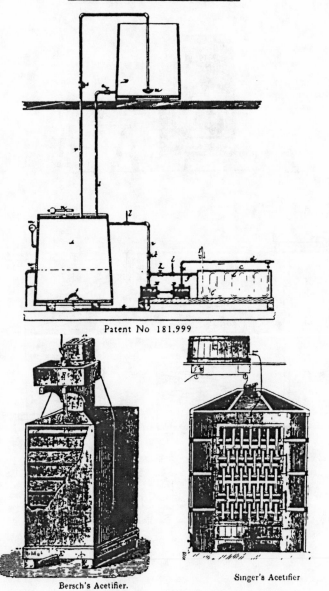

Patent No 181,999

Bersch's Acetifier.

Singer's Acetifier

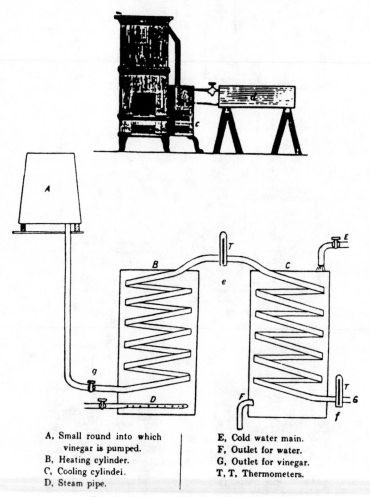

A, Small round into which
   vinegar is pumped.
B, Heating cylinder.
C, Cooling cylindei.
D, Steam pipe.

E, Cold water main.
F, Outlet for water.
G, Outlet for vinegar.
T, T, Thermometers.

Fig. 49.—Diagram of Sterilising Apparatus.

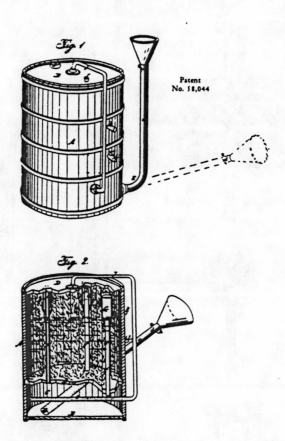

Fig. 1

Patent
No. 18,044

Fig. 2

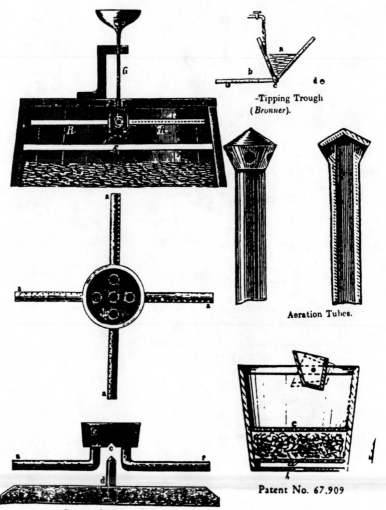

-Tipping Trough
(*Bronner*).

Aeration Tubes.

Patent No. 67,909

Sparge of an Acetifier (*Bronner*).

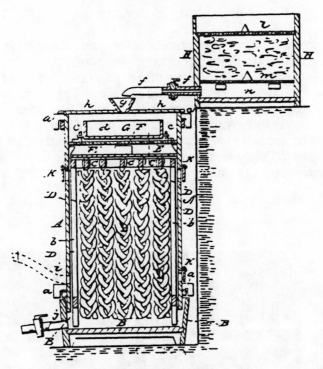

Patent No. 82,712

One of the areas of innovation to the quick process was the different kinds of packing materials used in the vinegar generator The materials included ceramics, charcoal, rattan, corn cobs, beechwood, coke, fir, cypress, oak, pine, redwood and many, many more. But though many more materials were studied, the packing of choice finally became beechwood shavings, due to the fact that these shavings could be used for up to 50 years without being replaced and imparted a pleasant taste to the product.

## Circulating generator

In 1929 another major improvement in the quick vinegar process was made. The circulating generator was introduced. Though the method is quite similar to other generator processes in principal, it has many distinct advantages. This circulating generator process can produce vinegars of higher acetic acid concentration than the previous methods. Tanks that require less space can be used. It also increases the vinegar production rate. These higher efficiencies are obtained by the use of forced aeration, continuous operation and tight control.over the entire process

## Submerged culture generation

Studies of submerged cultures were actually done as far back as 1923. The investigators looked at the use of pure cultures, the effect of the amount of innoculum, the forced aeration rate, the

temperature and the concentration of alcohol, as well as the uses of stimulants. They even looked at the action of various other bacteria on the acetification process.

It was not until the 1940s, however, that studies of methods of producing antibiotics paved the road for the actual production of vinegar by submerged culture. The submerged culture technique was probably most thoroughly studied in Austria, where the investigations went on for more than 14 years.[55] Hromatka and Ebner studied many facets of vinegar production, including the oxygen requirements of vinegar bacteria on beechwood shavings as well as the effects of pure oxygen on these bacteria. These studies encouraged other men to modify the submerged culture process.

## The Cavitator

One of the most significant modifications was the cavitator, a device that was developed for biological sewage treatment. This cavitator was first used for commercial vinegar production in the 1950s. Three different patents were granted from 1959 to 1961, but none of them overcame the many technical difficulties that finally forced the abandonment of the cavitator for vinegar production. However, the studies of the cavitator eventually led to the Frings acetator, which is still the state of the art in commercial vinegar production.

## The Frings acetator

The Frings acetator is fully automated and produces higher concentrations of acid than any of the other methods. The production rates and efficiencies also do not vary as widely as the older methods and equipment. The operation of this system is described in the production section.

FRINGS ACETATOR

Although the Frings acetator represents the state of the art in vinegar production today, new equipment and processes are continually being developed.

## SECTION TWO

## MAKING VINEGAR

In this section the reader will learn how vinegar is made in nature, in the home and in the factory. Starting with an explanation of the biochemical definition, all of the important elements of making all of the different kinds of vinegar will be discussed.

# CHAPTER 4

## UNDERSTANDING THE PROCESS

Before attempting to make vinegar, it is important to read this chapter carefully.

## THE BIOCHEMICAL DEFINITION
(See history section for legal definition.)

Acetic acid is the principal flavoring ingredient in vinegar. In fact, from a chemical viewpoint, vinegar is essentially nothing more than a weak solution of acetic acid in water with small amounts of various soluble extractive and mineral salts obtained from the raw materials used with by-products from the life processes of the organisms associated with vinegar manufacture. These extractives, salts, and by-products give the vinegar its distinctive flavor and determine its quality.

The making of vinegar is a biological process in which micro-organisms turn carbohydrates into acetic acid. It is usually referred to as a double fermentative process, staring with sugar $C_6H_{12}O_6$ and proceeding to alcohol and then to acetic acid or vinegar ($CH_3COOH$). However, in the case of rice wine vinegar, we start with a starch and proceed to sugar and then to alcohol and through to vinegar. In this case we refer to the process as a triple fermentative one. The process looks like this.

## DOUBLE FERMENTATION

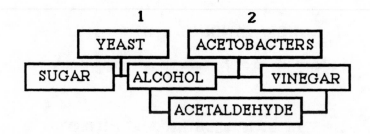

## TRIPLE FERMENTATION

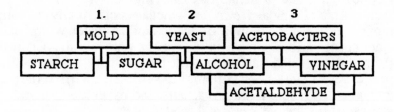

## HOW VINEGAR IS MADE

To make vinegar we need the bacteria that make the vinegar, the raw material for them to convert and suitable conditions in which they can live.

You may be surprised, even a little disturbed, that vinegar is produced by bacteria. If you are disturbed, be aware that bacteria are involved in the preparation of a large portion of the food we eat. Cheese, yogurt, wine, bread, pickles, chocolate, and coffee are just a few of the food items in which microorganisms are used to prepare. Foods like cheese and pickles are consumed with the live microorganisms. There are many microorganisms on which human life depends. *Acetobacter aceti* is only one of those microorganisms.

# ACETOBACTERS

> Dear God, what marvels there be in so small a creature.
>
> Leuenhooks
> Draftsman

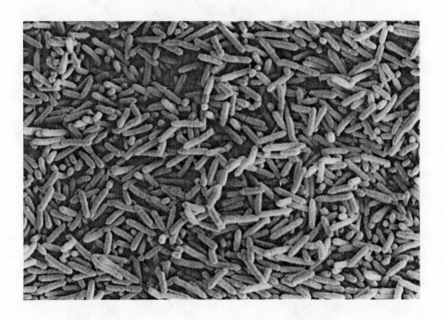

SCANNING ELECTRON MICROGRAPH OF ACETOBACTER

Vinegar is made by acetic acid bacteria principally known as acetobacters. These microorganisms are quite amazing. They are defined biologically as strictly aerobic(they need oxygen to live), and non-sporiferous (they do not form spores). They reproduce by duplicating themselves.

## ACETOBACTER IN VARIOUS STAGES OF DUPLICATION

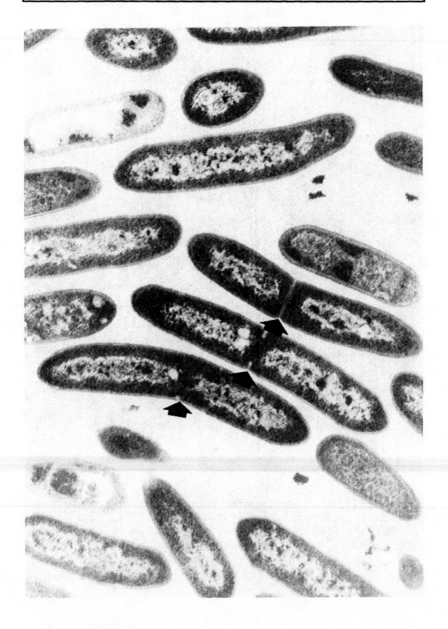

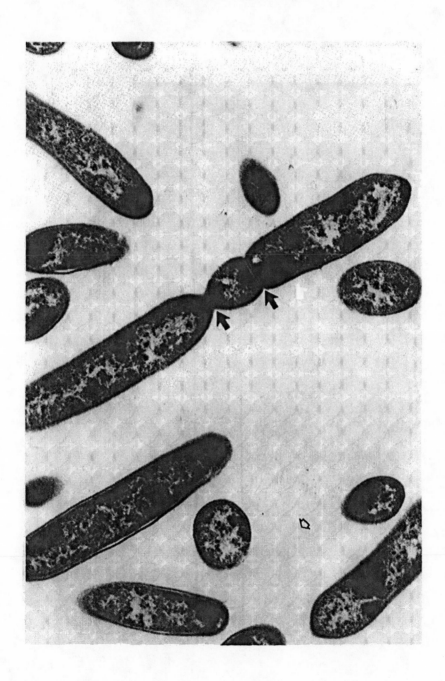

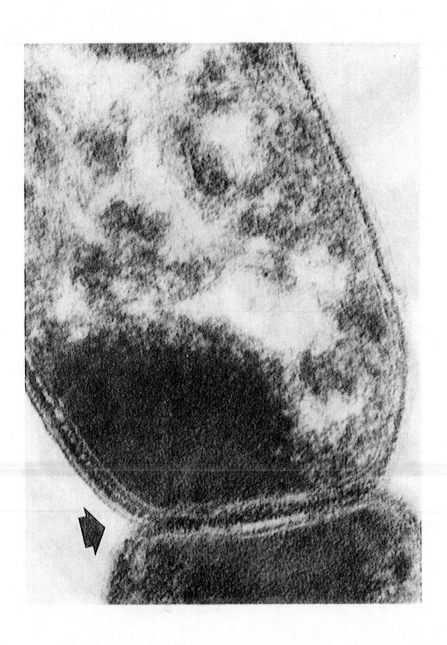

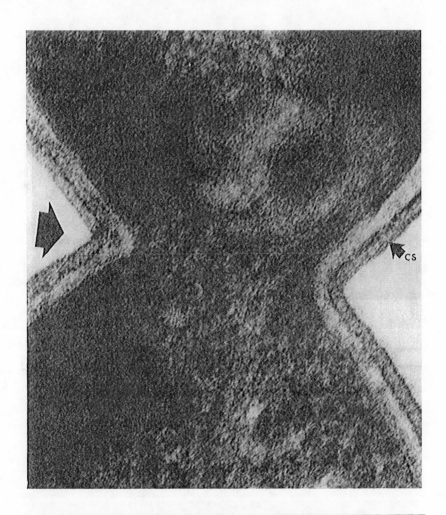

CLOSE UP OF ACETOBACTER SHOWING CYTOPLASMIC SAC (CS)

They are enclosed in a cytoplasmic sac which is a kind of skin for the bacteria.(**CS**) They are gram negative or gram variable (an important reaction to a special dye which is used to classify bacteria). They are pleomorphic, meaning that they can change their shape. They are usually rod-shaped.

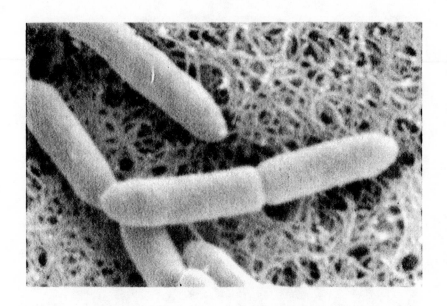

SCANNING ELECTRON MICROGRAPH OF ACETOBACTER

But they also often appear round, thread-like or in many other forms.

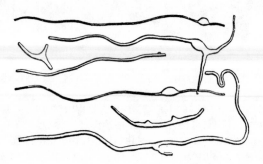

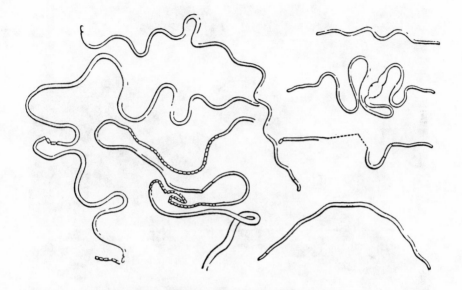

UNUSUAL FORMS OF ACETOBACTER

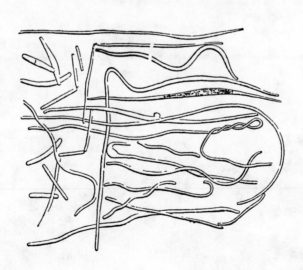

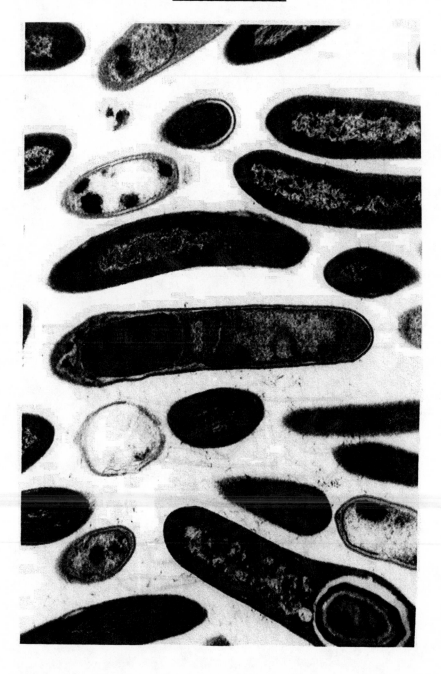

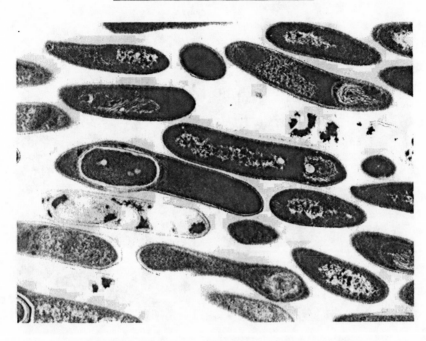

They are usually about 6 micrometers x 3 micrometers, but this can vary greatly, even in the same culture.

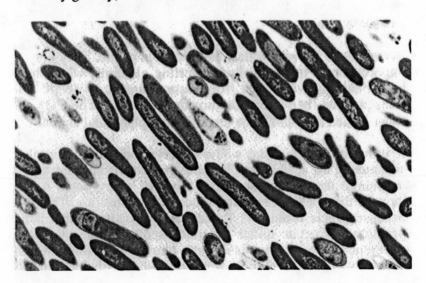

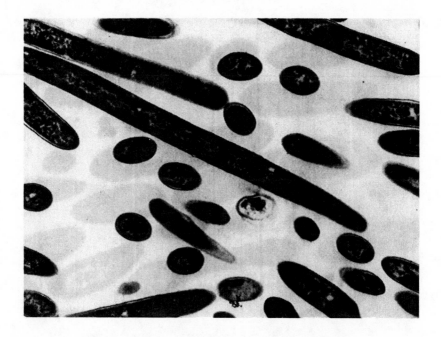

They are often motile (they can move by themselves), but their motility depends on age, oxygen supply, medium, etc. They move by means of a flagella, a whip-like appendage which looks like a tail.

Acetobacters are very widely distributed in nature. They play an important role in nature by converting alcohols, which have been made by wild yeast from natural sugars, to acetic acid (vinegar) and then to carbon dioxide and water. The $CO_2$ and water is then available to be used by other plants and animals.

It is important to make a few observations about the classification of the acetobacter. Because the bacteria have the ability to change their shape so drastically, for many years it was thought that there were many kinds of acetobacters. This was because when biologists looked at the bacteria that were producing vinegar under the microscope, they saw many different types of organisms (see photos and illustrations). Naturally they thought these were separate and distinct types of organisms and assigned them different species. In addition to changing their shape, these bacteria also have the ability to change the kinds of products they consume as well as the products they produce from this consumption. The absorption of gram stain is another major indicator in the classification of bacteria. This characteristic can also change in the acetobacter.

Though these bacteria fail the spore test, scientist have observed unexplained masses which have produced cells which have been described as swollen and club shaped.

The masses are shown here in various stages of development.

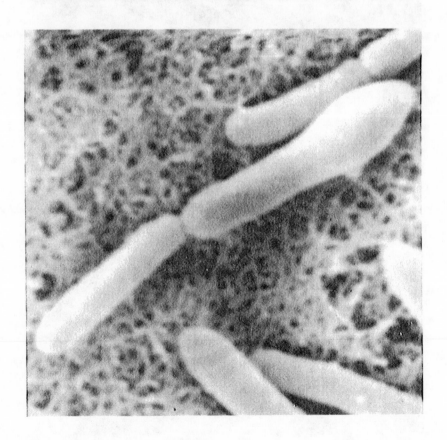

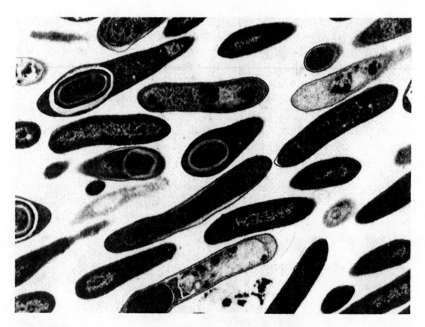

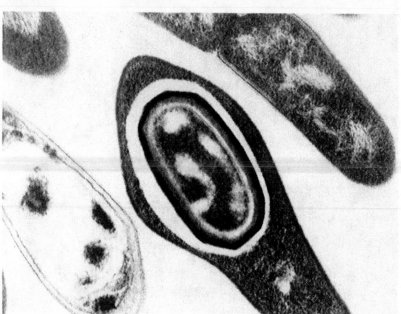

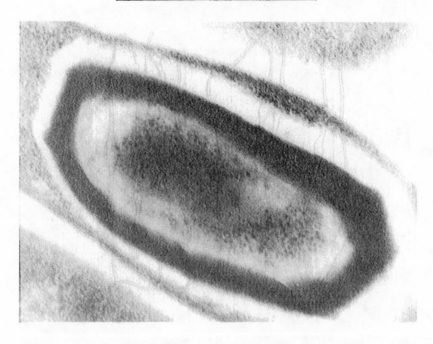

These cell forms ("Aberrations Formen " or "Involution Formen" were noticed by the first men to study the acetobacters (Hansen 1894).

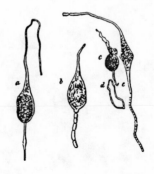

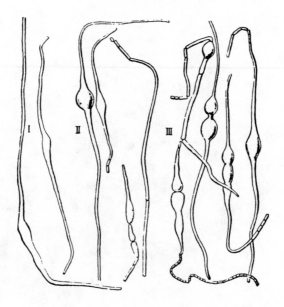

The reason for their appearance is not clearly understood, however it seems to be related to temperature, ph and media composition. In many cases 2 or more masses are found in some of the cells.

These masses are eventually liberated into the media or environment.

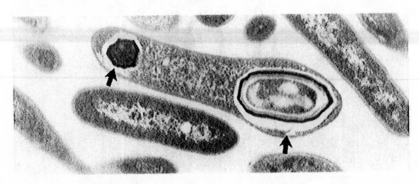

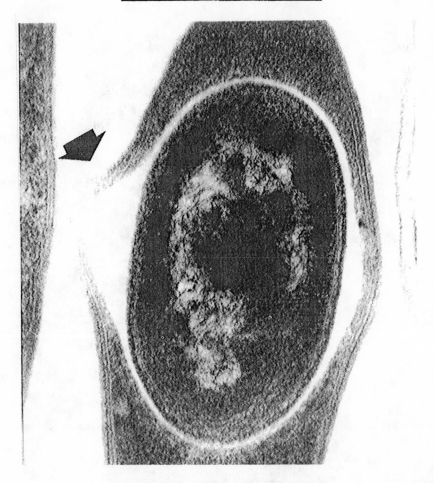

Note break in cytoplasmic sac just before release from cell

It has been postulated that these masses are part of the life cycle, (Janke 1916) but until now there has been no clear indication that this is the case. However when we look at some recent electron micrographs of these masses we see what appears to be genetic material.

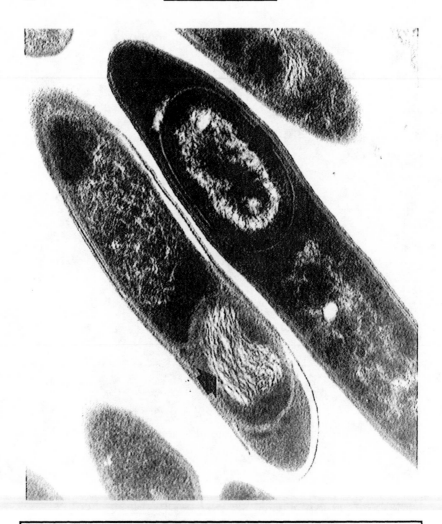

| NOTE EVIDENCE OF GENETIC MATERIAL |
| --- |

This suggests further that the acetobacter can use these masses to reproduce it self.

Since these masses are smaller than the vegetative or parent cell, they may be able to pass through the filters commonly used in the industry. And if it is more durable, as it appears to be, it can continue to exist under conditions (eg. the heat of pasteurization) which would normally kill the acetobacter. This may explain why wine which has been "cleaned up" suddenly and inexplicably becomes inoculated with this bacteria. It may also explain why it is so difficult to keep a mother from forming in vinegar which has been processed to avoid mothering.

Because biologist use these kinds of indicators to determine which species they are observing, for years they assumed that there were many species and variations of acetobacters. A lot of work went into isolating, classifying and documenting the various species. So don't be surprised if you find contradictions in literature that discusses the pros and cons of various species of acetobacters.

Historically, many different misconceptions about the acetobacters have been popular. In 1822, C.H. Persoon gave them the name Mycoderma, which means viscous film, because it appeared as a film like mat on top of the liquid that was turning into vinegar. In 1826 Desmazieres distinguished wine vinegars from beer vinegars by calling those that made wine vinegar *Mycoderma vine* and those that made beer vinegar *Mycoderma cerevesae*. Later, Kutzings called it *Ulvina aceti* because he thought it was a kind of algae. In 1852 Thompson later changed it to *Mycoderma aceti* because of the acetification the viscous film produced. During all of this time, scientists did not realize that bacteria were actually present but thought of them as one organism, the *Mycoderma* , roughly translated as the skin, or the mat.

In 1868, Louis Pasteur performed experiments and recorded some of the first in depth studies on the biology of vinegar production, but even he did not realize that bacteria were responsible for the production of vinegar and continued to refer to the *Mycoderma*. He did, however, show that it was the "*Mycoderma*" which was chiefly responsible for turning the famous and valuable French wines into vinegar.

In 1873, Knieriem and Mayer, became the first to identify the acetobacter. Cohen is also given credit for doing similar

experiments at around the same time. In 1879 Hansen classified
the bacteria into three different kinds. (see Hansen drawings)

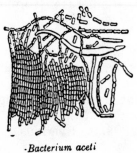

-*Bacterium aceti*
(after *Hansen*).

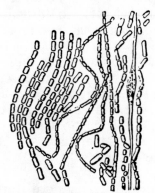

*Bacterium Pasteurianum*
(after *Hansen*).

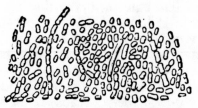

-*Bacterium Kützingianum*
(after *Hansen*).

| 1. Bacterium Aceti  2. B. Pasteurianum 3. B. Kutzingainum .[56] |
| --- |

Since that time a lot of controversy has developed around the
classification of the acetobacter. The controversy continues.

Recent research suggest that there are basically two kinds of
acetobacters. Some researchers believe that there may be only
one species of acetobacter.[57] J. L. Shimwell found that no
sooner had he isolated a strain of acetobacter that it would start
to change its biochemical and other characteristics. He noted that
in some cases the culture as a whole retained its particular

characteristics for a long time, but eventually those characteristics would wane until they were lost altogether. Sometimes one species would even take on the biochemical or other properties of other species. But most importantly many cultures would completely cease to correspond to the species they were originally found to be, and would even , on occasion, regain the original properties.

What is clear from the work of all of these scientists, especially Shimwell, is that any classification of the acetobacters past the level of genus is difficult , at best, to make.

This is important to the vinegar maker because it points out the uselessness of obtaining so-called pure species or strains of acetobacters. Earlier literature will suggest particular species and/or strains to be used with a warning to exclude all others. This effort is not worth the time or expense because of the forestated reasons. This also explains why it is difficult, if not impossible, to find an operating vinegar plant that contains a "pure species," They exist only in the laboratory and even then only for a relatively short time. So even if you do inoculate your vinegar still with a "pure strain," it will most likely change to something else soon after inoculation.

Although we are chiefly concerned with their ability to oxidize (add oxygen to) alcohol, we must remain keenly alert to the fact that acetobacters will oxidize acetic acid to carbon dioxide and water. This fact is very important to remember when making and storing vinegar.

## MOTHER OF VINEGAR

As mentioned before, the mat that is commonly found floating on the top of the fermenting vinegar is called the mother of vinegar. Also called the zoogloea, vinegar bees, vinegar mat and mycoderma.

## MOTHER GROWING IN BOTTLE

Historically, it was believed that vinegar could not be made without this mother. However, we now know that it is not necessary. As long as the acetobacter are alive in the proper solution, under the proper conditions, vinegar will be produced.

In some kinds of commercial production the mother is undesirable because it clogs up the machinery and slows down the process. It also means that the bacteria are converting the alcohol to cellulose instead of vinegar. So for many years an enormous amount of hours and dollars were spent developing special equipment and "pure strains" to overcome this mothering "problem."

It remains a constant source of frustration for the sellers of vinegar whose customers think that the sediment of mother in the bottle is a contaminate. If this mothering means anything, it is a sign that the vinegar is pure enough to support the growth of the acetobacter. If the contents of the bottle is indeed vinegar and more than 4 percent acetic acid, it is highly unlikely that there are any other living organisms in the bottle except acetobacters. This mother can be easily filtered out to improve the aesthetics.

This mother of vinegar takes on many forms. Sometimes it is thick and sometimes it is thin. It may float on the top of the ferment or it may ascend from the bottom like seaweed from the ocean floor. The surface may be smooth or textured. The colors range from transparent to dark brown or even black. Sometimes it is made up of cellulose and other times of complex sugars.

> These photos show fresh / live mother taken from fermenting vinegar.

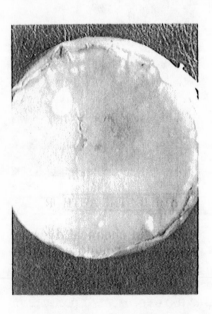 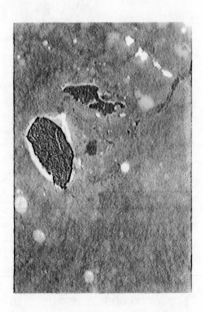

A light wooden grating or raft is sometimes used as a support for the mother in the vinegar still to keep it from falling to the bottom and rotting. In the quick fermentation processes the mother often grows on the, beechwood shavings or chips, rattan, charcoal, coke, corn cobs, or pumice which is used for packing material. This will cause the machinery to clog and production will slow down considerably.

The mother of vinegar may in the near future have another use. Because of its cellulose fiber content, it can be used to make a kind of cloth or paper

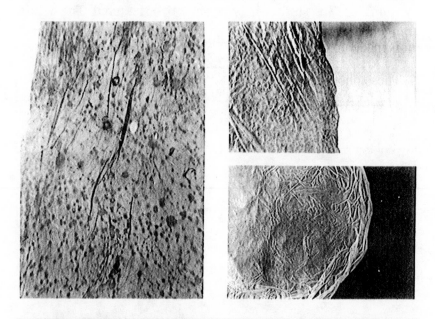

PHOTOS OF VINEGAR PAPER MADE BY THE AUTHOR

Researchers have found that when certain chemical dyes are added to the environment of the bacteria, the cellulose fibers in the mother will widen and can even be used to make a reasonably strong cloth. The reason that this cloth has not been produced commercially is that it is too expensive to produce in usable quantities.

## OPTIMUM CONDITIONS FOR MAKING VINEGAR

For the vinegar bacteria to convert alcohol into acetic acid, they need certain conditions.

## RAW MATERIALS FOR MAKING VINEGAR

Vinegar can be made from almost any vegetation containing sugar. In fact, about 10 percent of vinegar is made from wood! The wood sugar; from the processing of paper provides the raw material for much of the industrial vinegar made in the the United States. This vinegar is often referred to as Georgia Pacific vinegar because so much of the sugar comes from this giant paper company.

## CONCENTRATION OF ALCOHOL

The simplest way to make vinegar is to start from alcohol. The care exercised in the choice of suitable alcohol will play a crucial role in the quality and taste of the resulting vinegar. Some alcoholic mixtures present certain problems of conversion that are difficult to overcome. Pure ethyl alcohol and water produce a colorless vinegar that doesn't have the agreeable aromatic substances that give value to fine vinegars. This kind of vinegar finds wide industrial use. All other alcohols used for making vinegar bring with them inherent qualities that will change the quality of the vinegar made from them. Many different alcoholic mixtures have been tried, and some are commonly used to make vinegar.

Adjustment of the alcoholic concentration of the vinegar stock may be necessary to assure successful acetification (See Technical Data Appendix for calculation directions). The amount of alcohol present should not be so high that the acetobacters cannot function normally. It must also not be so low that the finished vinegar will be below useful or, in the case of commercial production, legal requirements in strength. The liquid solution should contain an alcohol level of 5 percent to 12 percent. Alcohol concentrations of higher than 15 percent inhibit the growth of acetobacters and may even kill them, while concentrations lower than 5 percent may cause over-oxidation and a subsequent loss of vinegar. Alcohol concentrations of 9 percent to 12 percent is readily fermented. But the optimum is approximately 10 percent

## MAKING VINEGAR FROM "SCRATCH"

To obtain the most control over the final product, it is necessary to make the vinegar from scratch". Many different raw materials are being used and, no doubt, some that are possible have not yet been tried (see Raw Materials appendix for more information).

The raw materials commonly used to make vinegar can be divided into four groups: cereals, fruit juices, sugar syrups, and industrial ethyl alcohol. The procedure followed for making vinegar from these will vary due to differences of the chemical composition of each.

## VINEGARS FROM FRUIT JUICES

Vinegars are commonly derived from a wide variety of fruit juices, including those from apples, grapes, oranges, peaches, pears, apricots, berries, bananas, watermelons and persimmons. In fact, any fruit juice containing enough sugar will produce an acceptable vinegar, provided it is not otherwise objectionable. Of course, the fruit used should be clean, sound and mature. In the conversion of sugar to alcohol by fermentation, 100 parts of sugar in the juice should theoretically produce about 51 parts of alcohol; i.e., about half as much alcohol by weight should be obtained as there was sugar in the juice[58]. In actual practice, you can get only 43 percent to 47 percent, because some of the sugar is used by the yeasts and other organisms for purposes other than alcohol production. In converting alcohol into acetic acid, 100 parts of alcohol should theoretically give 130 parts of acetic acid, but actually less than 120 parts are obtained because certain other bacteria and yeasts which are most likely to be present, also use alcohol as food.

So under favorable conditions, for every 100 parts of sugar present 50 to 55 parts of acetic acid should be produced. This means that if you want a vinegar containing 5.2 percent acetic acid, the fermentation should be started with at least a 10 percent sugar solution, while for a 4.1 percent acetic acid content, the sugar solution should contain at least 8.2 percent sugar.

The choices of fruit juices that may be used for vinegar production will tend to be limited by these factors. If, as in the case of watermelons, the juices contain less than 5.2 percent sugar, they must be concentrated by boiling or evaporation. On the other hand, if they contain much more than 14 percent sugar, like persimmons or raisins, they must be diluted.

## CEREAL VINEGAR

Those making fruit juice vinegars have an advantage over those making cereal vinegars in that they don't have to convert the starch of their product into sugar. This is one reason why fruit juice vinegars are sometimes cheaper than cereal vinegars like those obtained from malts.

The component of cereals most important the vinegar maker is starch, which is present in large amounts. This must first be converted to sugars by; the action of malting; acids or enzymes. The enzymes usually come from molds. The sugars are then fermented to alcoholic spirits by yeasts and the ethyl alcohol turned into acetic acid by vinegar bacteria. If molds are used to convert the starch to sugar, this becomes a triple fermentation process.

Malt vinegar is a good example of vinegar originating from cereals. In the past, sour beer provided almost all of the malt vinegar. But the science of brewing has made the beer industry so efficient that sour beer is scarce. As a result, the malt vinegar manufacturer must rely on specially prepared worts. ( A wort is an infusion of sugars from starchy cereals in water, prepared by mashing but before fermentation to an alcohol). The advantage here is that it is now possible to have a uniform and biologically clean source of sugars.

Corn sugar vinegar is another example of a vinegar originating from cereals[59]. The corn sugar is obtained by chemical treatment of corn starch. The starch from other cereals may also be converted and used this way.

In countries where it is abundant, rice is used for the making of vinegar. The making of rice vinegar has evolved into an art form in Japan and China.

The conversion of rice starch into sugar in the natural process of making vinegar is usually done using a mold called *Aspergillus oryzae*. The enzymes produced by this mold change the starch into sugar. This mold is also used to make many other food products in the orient. There is also a commercially prepared powdered enzyme that will perform quite well if the mold itself is unavailable or undesired. This powder is considerably easier to use. Instructions for using this enzyme and the mold *Aspergillus oryzae.* is beyond the scope of this book (see Suppliers of Materials appendix for sources of the enzyme and the mold as well as instructions for their use).

Rice vinegar is often erroneously called rice <u>wine</u> vinegar. Wine is, technically speaking, made from fruit. Since rice is a grain, no wine of any kind can result from its use. But if the error persists, we may need to change the definition of wine.

## VINEGAR FROM ROOTS

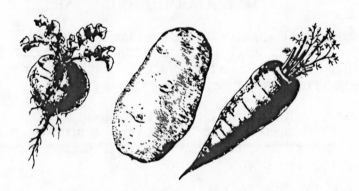

Irish potatoes, yams and sweet potatoes also contain starch that can be used to make vinegar. The processes followed are very close to those followed when grain is the source of starch. Potato vinegar, which is reported to be widely used in Germany, is an example . Irish potatoes usually contain from 16 percent to 22 percent starch [60], but because of the unpopular taste of fermented Irish potatoes, vinegar from them is usually made from alcohol that has been distilled from them rather than from the fermented mash directly.

Sweet potatoes usually contain 25 percent to 30 percent of total starches and sugars. Although most of this is starch, the combined total can be turned into vinegar. Sweet potatoes will make a palatable, though not award-winning, vinegar without distillation.

## SYRUP VINEGARS

Like fruit juices, syrups contain the sugars and other ingredients necessary for making vinegar. The general process followed in converting them is therefore similar in principle. Honey, maple products, molasses and whey have all been used (see raw materials appendix for brief notes on various raw materials).

## ETHYL ALCOHOL VINEGARS

Industrial ethyl alcohol is the most important materials for the production of vinegar from an economic viewpoint. In the United States, Georgia Pacific or GP alcohol makes up about 10 percent of the raw material source for vinegar.

According to Don Mc Intyre, Vice President of Manufacturing for Fleishmanns Vinegar, "Distilled vinegar in the United States is produced from one of three sources of alcohol, 1. synthetic, 2. grain, and 3. wood.

"Price has generally determined which source of alcohol is used although in the last few years there has been a movement toward "natural" alcohols -the grain and wood. Synthetic alcohol probably has nearly 50 percent of the total market today; grain probably 40 percent and wood 10 percent.

"The quality of all three alcohols is identical and are virtually indistinguishable from the vinegar manufacturers view point." We switch sources as prices change and see no difference in production, yield or vinegar quality.

"Synthetic alcohol is often "purer" than "natural" alcohols as it is refined to a higher degree and has none of the fermentation by products. These differences however are slight and due to only trace amounts of esters and aldehydes. The major producers of synthetic alcohol are Union Carbide, USI and Eastman. Their raw material source is ethylene from natural gas.

"Grain alcohol is produced in the mid-west from corn and wheat. This alcohol source has become more popular in the last 5 years due to the "natural" aspect which has been given considerable market attention by Heinz. Prices of grain have been favorable to this promotion and many producers have switched to tout a "natural' product. However, the only way to tell the difference between a grain alcohol and a synthetic alcohol is to test the products for radioactive carbon isotopes. This "carbon dating" technique is new and only done by two labs in the U.S.

"Grain alcohol is produced by Grain Processing, Mid-West Grain and Archer-Daniels Midland (ADM).

"Wood alcohol produced by Georgia Pacific in Bellingham, Washington is generally sold only on the west coast and must compete with synthetic alcohol and grain alcohol as well.

"A small amount of molasses alcohol is imported for east coast vinegar producers. Again, this product is of similar quality to all the others and can be substituted without problem. The volume is so small today that it can be considered insignificant. In past years however, molasses sourced alcohol was a major raw material for vinegar manufacturers. This is a good example of how economic conditions dictate the alcohol sources."

## VINEGAR BACTERIA FOODS

Like yeast, acetobacters need more than a single basic nutrient to thrive. Although the nutritional requirements of these organisms have not been studied as intensively as those of the industrially important yeasts, it has been established that the acetobacters will not grow well without certain inorganic salts like potassium tartrate, ammonium phosphate and ammonium chloride. This was made clear during studies on the manufacture of honey vinegar[61]. Honey contains only small amounts of inorganic salts, and the nutritional deficit becomes pronounced unless something is done to supplement these needs of the bacteria. Usually fruit juices and similar substances contain enough of the inorganic needed salts to make further additions unnecessary. But when industrial ethyl alcohol is being converted to vinegar, appropriate bacterial foods must be added because industrial ethyl alcohol is so pure that it contains virtually no other components except alcohol and water.

Sour Beer is often used to supply the important nutrients of acetobacters when converting industrial alcohol into acetic acid. One gallon of sour beer for every 100 gallons of alcohol is the usual mixture. It is important to use only freshly boiled sour beer to prevent contamination by microorganisms that are often found in beer.

Sweet unhopped malt wort may also be used at about the same proportion as sour beer, but it is usually too expensive to be of use commercially.

Malt extract and dried malt preparations contain a higher nutrient content, so smaller amounts- 200 grams per 100 liters of industrial alcohol- are recommended[62].

Frings Extract is a secret formula that was worked out after many years of experience. It is marketed under the name Acetozym. One and a half kilograms of this nutrient is added to 1,000 liters of mash that contains 12.8 percent to 13 percent alcohol. [63]

Low-quality wines may also be used at the rate of one gallon per 100 gallons of ethyl alcohol. But care must be taken to make sure that the liquid does not contain harmful microorganisms or harmful chemicals.

Yeast concentrations that have been properly sterilized or broths prepared by extraction of yeast masses in water seem to work very well as acetobacter nutrients. Yeast is obtained as a by product of alcoholic fermentation, so yeast broth is a relatively cheap and effective source of nutrients. The amount to be used will largely depend on how the preparation was made, so it is difficult to make a recommendation as to how to use it. However, a little experimentation should should provide the answer to this question.

Molasses contains quite a bit of organic and inorganic yeast nutrients. Two hundred to 300 grams per 100 liters of industrial alcohol are ordinarily used to promote acetic fermentation.

Vitamin B-1, in small amounts, has been found to speed up the production of acetic acid fermentation.[64]

# PHYSICAL ENVIRONMENT
## TEMPERATURE

Temperature control is critical in producing a commercial vinegar which is economically competitive. It is also important, though not as critical, to the hobbyist.

Vinegar is produced at temperatures between 59-94 degrees Fahrenheit. Temperatures below 59 degrees Fahrenheit cause the production rate to fall too low. As temperatures rise above 94 degrees F. production begins to fall. The bacteria will be killed at 140 degrees. F.

Acetobacters exhibit very definite and bizarre changes with temperature changes. Between 54 degrees F and 59 degrees F., the organism grows very slowly and the cells are short but unusually broad. Between 59 degrees F and 94 degrees P, they appear to develop in what may be called a " normal " manner, growing rapidly and developing their cells in chains. When proper foods foods for them are available, the walls become swollen and exhibit the early stages of mother formation

As temperatures rise even higher (approximately from 107 degrees F to 130 degrees F.), they appear as long and thread like, transparent filaments, often with no cross walls. Irregular bulging and certain as-yet-undefined masses also form. These masses seem to contain the genetic material of the acetobacter (see electron micro photos). Occasional branching have also been seen. This seems to be an undesirable condition brought on by high temperature, and if the culture is kept in this condition very long, the organisms may permanently lose their ability to function normally. If they are quickly returned to temperatures of from 59 degrees F. to 94 degrees F., however, some cells of normal appearance and behavior will be produced from which a new culture will develop.

This unusual temperature effect is useful as a temperature indicator for active acetification in vinegar manufacture.

The exact temperature to be used will depend on the organism in the process being employed. A temperature of 8O degrees F. to 85 degrees F. is usually optimum for acetification.[65] As in alcohol fermentation, if the temperature is too low, the rate of acetification is very slow. A temperature that is too high promotes losses through evaporation of alcohol, acetic acid and the volatile substances that impart the subtle flavor and aroma of fine vinegar.

But here also there is at least a bit of controversy. In England, for example, somewhat higher acetification temperatures are used than in United States. C.A, Mitchell's "Vinegar: Its Manufacture and Examination," states that a temperature of from 103 degrees F. to 110 degrees F. is the usual practice there. Experience will ultimately be your best guide.

# WATER

Pure water is a very important prerequisite for making vinegar. Hard water tends to retard the vinegar production process. Also carbonates of lime, magnesium, etc. tend to neutralize some of the acid. Water that contains organic matter will tend to deteriorate the quality of fine vinegar. If iron is found in the water, it will unite with the tannins in the vinegar and produce a very inky-looking color

The softer the water is, the better it is for making vinegar. Pure, soft and clear spring water has the highest recommendation. When this is not available, purified well or spring water will do. Distilled water can also be recommended. When all of these are impossible, impractical or too expensive, filtered water may be used successfully.

Many city water supplies are chlorinated or fluoridated. These products are antibiotic and can disrupt fermentation even when present in minute quantities. Other elements that are common in city water, organic as well as inorganic, can alter the vinegar production process.

# CLEANLINESS

As in any process that is biological in nature, cleanliness is very important. Many different kinds of microorganisms coexist with us all of the time. Many of these are undesirable organisms that can and will take over the solutions of starch, sugar or alcohol much faster than the desirable organisms if we are not careful. So it is very important to clean all of the equipment and utensils that will be used for vinegar making. The vinegar still and the storage space must also be clean and orderly. Not only should everything be clean, but anything that will inhibit fermentation or cause undesirable tastes or odors should be avoided. Of course, barrels and containers that have been used to store paints, oils, varnishes or industrial alcohol should never be used for making vinegar.

Household bleach can be recommended for cleaning the utensils and working space, but it is important to thoroughly rinse the bleach away since it is as toxic to the desirable organisms as to the undesirable ones. Steam can also be used destroy unwanted microorganisms, insects and nematodes (worms) that are common pests when making vinegar.

## MATERIALS FOR EQUIPMENT AND UTENSILS

When selecting the equipment, tools, and utensils to make vinegar, certain ground rules must be kept in mind. Vinegar must be kept out of contact with most metals at all times. Aluminum, copper, lead, zinc and iron are particularly dangerous. They will react with the vinegar and aesthetically ruin or poison it. The only metal that can be tolerated in the making of vinegar is high-grade stainless steel. Remember, since matter can neither be created nor destroyed, when you see corrosion on the utensils used for making vinegar it is logical to assume that the material that has disappeared has gone somewhere. In this case, it is probably into your vinegar.

Cement is also to be avoided (see photos of cement damage).

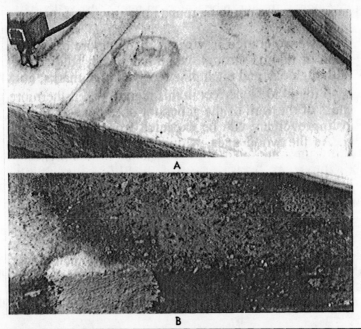

A. Before attack by acetic acid   B. After attack by acetic acid

As seen in these photos, vinegar will dissolve cement. And although it is one of the best materials to use for flooring, you must expect that you will need to resurface the floor periodically because the vinegar vapors will eat away the surface. A good quality paint, asphalt or epoxy coating will slow the corrosion process considerably.

Some materials that can be recommended are wood, bamboo, ceramics (with non-metal finish), glass, enamel and, in a pinch, food-grade plastic, food-grade fiber glass or hard rubber. The woods selected from the Woods for Aging appendix have a history of usage in the wine and vinegar industries. They will add flavors and aromas to your vinegars in addition to acting as a safe utensil. Of course, you should want the aroma or taste they impart. Pine, for example, is used to flavor some wines, but those wines are not to be found on many best-seller lists.

The losses encountered in vinegar manufacture caused by the diffusion of liquids through wood have been studied closely. And although oak and pitch pine received high marks, no wood has been found to be perfect in this regard.[66]. Furthermore, the thickness of the wall of the generator does not seem to matter, so no improvement can be expected from the use of thicker wood. As the wood ages, it quickly becomes more porous, indicating that that even when the generators are structurally sound, they may be losing great quantities of alcohol and vinegar. A new generator may lose up to a 1/4 of a liter per day[67] If the generators are made of earthenware, these loses can be cut slightly.[68]

It should be mentioned that the makers of balsamic vinegar, one of the worlds finest vinegars, choose some of their woods precisely because they allow evaporation. This evaporation is the mechanism used to condense the vinegar to its syrupy-like consistency.

Barrels and containers that have been used for making alcohol brandy, whiskey or wine are very good for making vinegar. They will often enhance the quality of your vinegar.

Glass, ceramics, baked enamels and food-grade plastics are also used for vessels to hold the mixtures. They have the advantage of being easier to sterilize than wood. If the aroma of the wood is desired, wood chips can be added with good results. Bamboo, rubber, glass and plastics are used for pipes and tubes.

## LIGHT

Vinegar fermentation will proceed best in a place that eliminates ultraviolet light. Most bacteria are sensitive to UV light and acetobacters are no different (see chart on the relationship of colored glass to growth rate of the bacteria)

EFFECT OF FILTERED LIGHT ON ACETIC ACID PRODUCTION IN VINEGAR

From the chart, however, we can see that the process will continue even when there is a considerable amount of ultraviolet light. So, although total darkness is desirable almost any container will work. Another method of handling this problem, at the hobbyist level, is to put the vinegar in a dark room, cabinet or sack.

## OXYGEN

The bacteria need a readily available source of oxygen. Adding oxygen to alcohol is how the bacteria make vinegar. The oxygen can come right from the air but must be readily available. All other factors being equal, the more oxygen provided, the faster the rate of production. Most of the major patents taken out on vinegar making apparatus have been in some way aimed at making more oxygen available to the bacteria. There are so many ways to make oxygen available to the bacteria that the only limitation here seems to be ingenuity.

## MOTION

The vinegar generator, or still, as well as the aging container should be stationary. Movement of the still in the slow process will tend to retard production. It may also cause the mother to fall to the bottom and rot in the tank. A fallen mother will deteriorate the quality of the vinegar. If the vinegar is moved during the aging period, the sediments that have settled will be stirred up again, causing a loss of one of the major benefits of aging.

## TIME

Time is one of the most important elements in vinegar making. In large scale commercial manufacture, "time is money," so the faster they can convert the alcohol to vinegar the more money they can make. The banks look very favorably on this. While the slow, or Orleans, methods may take four to six months to make vinegar, the acetator may produce that same quantity of vinegar in 48 hours or less.

For the vinegar maker who seeks the highest quality product, just the opposite is true...to a point. It seems that when the acetobacters are allowed to work their magic at an unhurried pace, the quality of the product is greatly enhanced. This method produces a very heavy, rich, smooth product that is preferred by gourmets the world over. Long aging periods also add to the subtle aromas and tastes that separate ordinary vinegars from superior ones. The value of these products also increases, so the gain in intrinsic value over time compensates in a large degree for the initial losses.

The slow process also carries with it more risks than the quicker methods. There is greater control over the quick automated processes than the slow processes. The more time it takes, the more time there is for things to foul up. There is also more labor involved per gallon than the quick method. This means that the cost of producing this product is greatly increased. Incidentally, this is why good vinegar costs more and is worth more than good wine.

# VINEGAR TESTING

If you are not planning to be a serious vinegar maker, then it really isn't important to acquire all of the equipment and chemicals necessary to accurately test vinegar. After all, people were making vinegar long before any of this testing equipment was available. However, if you intend to consistently make high-quality vinegar either as a hobby or for sale, you will definitely need to get good, reliable equipment to test your vinegar, as well as the raw materials.

You will need apparatus for testing the sugar, alcohol, acetic acid level and the taste of your vinegar. This equipment and the instructions for making the test may be readily obtained from good wine-making and or beer-making supply shops, and for the hobbyist, some of it can be found in the home (see the Suppliers of Materials appendix for sources of supply).

There are two basic ways to determine if the vinegar has reached its desired acetic acid content. One is the complete disappearance of alcohol by the smell or taste test. Unless you are planning to be a serious vinegar maker, this will work fine. It was the only method for thousands of years. The other is to chemically test it by titration. Titration kits come with instructions for their use and are available from amateur wine and beer making shops.

# VINEGAR STORAGE AND AGING

## STORAGE OF VINEGAR

One of the chief causes of the deterioration of vinegar is the bacteria that make the vinegar. If left exposed to air in the absence of alcohol, these bacteria will then convert the vinegar into carbon dioxide and water. So whereas the presence of air was crucial in the acetification process, it is now, to the same degree, undesirable. The acid level will begin to fall after it has reached its peak. When it has fallen to 2 percent or lower, other microorganisms will now begin to take over. At this point all is lost.

To prevent this unfortunate turn of events, the container should be filled completely to the top. It should be corked and then sealed with wax. A screw type cap may also be used provided it has a new seal on the inside of the cap.

Vinegar should be stored in a cool, 40 to 50 degrees F., dry place for at least six months. The longer the vinegar is stored, the better it will be. High temperatures tend to decompose the vinegar. The addition of a small percentage of alcohol into vinegar that is being stored, particularly during aging, tends to improve the keeping quality of the vinegar.

# AGING

Fresh vinegar has a very sharp and biting taste. Its true quality is best revealed by aging. During aging, it becomes more mellow. The esters and ethers of the vinegars are allowed to mature, and many of the finer qualities emerge. A minimum of six months is required for vinegar to begin to attain its highest qualities. The longer it is aged, the more these subtle qualities will appear.

AGING VINEGAR AT
KIMBERLY VINEGAR WORKS IN SAN FRANCISCO

Aging should be carried out in a tightly sealed container that has been filled to the top with vinegar. The esters and ethers of woods will greatly enhance the character of the vinegar (see Woods for Aging appendix for suggestions of woods to use). If wooden barrels are used to store the vinegar, then all that is needed is for the barrel to be completely filled. However, if glass containers are used for storage, it is suggested that you, select woods listed in the Woods for Aging appendix, make some large chips or shavings (not saw dust) and add one unpacked cup of this per gallon of vinegar.

More wood can be added if you want. You might also try combinations of various woods as is done in the production of balsamic vinegar. The variations in taste and aromas are limited only by your imagination. The cost should be minimal. The great balsamics (see chapter 9) get much of their unique qualities from the process of transferring the vinegar to barrels made from various kinds of wood. Each wood contributes its unique characteristic to the vinegar, and years later what began as a melody becomes a symphony.

Another reason that aging is important is that it gives the vinegar a chance to settle which improves the visual qualities. In many cases, vinegars which are not clear when the fermentation has ended will become clear while aging.

## CLEANING UP THE VINEGAR

## RACKING OFF

After the vinegar has aged sufficiently, it should be racked off. This should be done carefully so that you don't disturb the sediment that has accumulated on the bottom. This racking off should be done with as little exposure to air as possible (see diagram).

This process should be repeated if your are going to age the vinegar for a long period of time.

If this vinegar is only for home use and appearance is not critical, this process will produce an adequately clear product. But to polish your vinegar you will need to consider clarifying it.

## CLARIFYING THE VINEGAR

Customarily, vinegars offered for sale are quite clear and brilliant. However, this clarification is only cosmetic and could be detrimental to the taste and aroma of the finished product if it is done poorly. It is also another expense that is unnecessary for the novice. So filtration and fining is not highly recommended unless you are going to enter you vinegar in contest where appearance is a factor or you will offer it for sale.

The difficulty in obtaining a bright and clear product will largely depend on the product from which the vinegar originated. Some juices, like that from apples, have a tendency to clear during fermentation. Others, like that from peaches, which contain a lot of pulp, are very difficult to clear. Vinegar made in acetators contain many fine particles and colloidal substances that are held in suspension along with the bacteria and their products that cause it to become extremely cloudy. So it is sometimes necessary to actually filter the vinegar to get a clear and bright product.

## FILTRATION

Vinegar can be clarified by filtration alone if the filtering equipment and materials are of the best quality. The standard method is to add diatamaceous earth to the vinegar and then pump it through a filter.

FILTERS FOR FILTERING LARGE VOLUMES OF VINEGAR

Diatamaceous earth is the outer shell of the diatom, a microscopic sea organism, that is made of calcium carbonate. It will remove particles that are 5 microns or larger. Additionally, filter pads , which are made of cellulose flock, are used. These filter pads will remove particles .2 microns or larger. This is, in effect, sterile vinegar since most micro-organisms are larger than this.

The vinegar may be further improved by passing it through porous porcelain filters. But the vinegar must have been already filtered or fined when this kind of unit is used, otherwise the filters will soon become clogged and cease to operate.

For small-scale operations,filtration kits can be obtained from wine-making supply houses. They work on the same principles as the larger operations and will work quite well for clarifying small amounts of vinegar.

## FINING

Fining is a very old process that has been used with beers and wines as well as vinegars. It has now largely been replaced by filtration, which accomplishes the same purpose in less time and with less trouble. But it is still used, so it is worth noting.

Good-quality bentonite is very popular in some circles for fining vinegar. It is an inert volcanic ash that imparts little or no taste and is relatively quick-acting.[69]. Some people also like Isinglass. It is made from the cleaned and dried swimming bladders of sturgeon or other fresh water fish[70]. Other materials such as gelatin, tannin[71], potassium ferrocyanide casein and powdered dried blood[72] have also been used to different degrees of success.

## PASTURIZATION

Pasteurization can also be considered as one of the important measures that can be taken to preserve the quality and strength of vinegar. Since the main cause of the deterioration of vinegar is the continued activities of the acetobacters, destroying them will eliminate their contribution to spoilage.

Even after filtering and clarifying the vinegar the acetobacters will continue to multiply and cause clouding or mothering. While this cloudiness and mothering does not in itself mean that the vinegar is deteriorating, it is usually a sign that the vinegar is being oxidized, even if very slowly, by the acetobacters.

To take care of this little problem, the temperature of the vinegar is raised from 140 to 160 degrees F. This effectively destroys the vinegar culture. It is important to note here that after this pasteurization, the vinegar should be closed of before the temperature drops. Otherwise the vinegar could become reinoculated with acetobacters floating in the air. However, for reasons already mentioned, this method is not foolproof.

The minimum effective temperature at which the pasteurization of vinegar can take place is 140 degrees F. On the other hand, if the temperature of the vinegar is raised above 160 degrees F, the acetic acid will began to evaporate. This will mean a loss of acetic acid strength as well as flavor and aroma.

## CONCENTRATING VINEGAR

Sometimes the vinegar manufacturer may want to concentrate the vinegar. The concentration of the vinegar allows for reduced storage space. Concentrated vinegars are also used in the pickling industry to deal with the problem of dilution when preserving large quantities of vegetables that contain large amounts of water.

In order to accomplish this, the vinegar is frozen and the water removed by filtering or centrifuging

## BOTTLING

It is quite common to allow the vinegar to remain in the still, generator or the bottle in which it was made. But this is not a good idea because it permits the entrance of air and interferes with the settling process.

When the aging and other desired processes are finished, the vinegar is ready for use. The clear vinegar should be syphoned off slowly so as not to disturb any sedimentation on the bottom or material floating on the top. The bottling should be done all at one time, using every precaution to minimize the vinegar's exposure to air.

It should then be bottled into small containers. Pint-sized containers with long, thin necks are recommended because they are easy to handle and provide for minimum exposure to air. The small containers also allow the vinegar to be used a little at a time without exposing the larger quantity to the air. But any kind of small-necked glass container that will minimize surface exposure will work well. The most important consideration is that the containers are completely filled and tightly sealed. Waxing is highly advantageous.

Some consideration to decorative bottles should be given. If they are old bottles, make sure they are sterilized before filling. This addition will make a great contribution to the presentation of your product, which tends to prejudice the user toward the contents.

Screw-type closures can be recommended if the cap has a new seal inside. Waxing in this case is not mandatory but would not hurt. Corks also work well. They should be inserted completely into the bottle with a corking device. This device can be found in wine-making supply shops. In this case sealing with wax is a must.

## WAXING

Wax for sealing the vinegar can be found in wine-making supply shops. If this wax cannot be found, sealing wax from stationary stores, parafin for canning or candle wax may be used successfully.

Melt the wax in a tall can or some other throw-away metal container that has been placed in a pan with a small amount of water. Heat the assembly over a low heat until it has a liquid consistency. Run a short length of ribbon up one side of the neck of the bottle, over the mouth and down the other side. Glue this piece of ribbon in place before dipping. This will allow the wax to be easily opened. Dip the bottle into the liquid wax and remove. This action may be required several times before the bottle is fully coated. The bottle may be further dressed with the addition of you own special label.

## LABELING

Once your vinegar has been packaged, it should be labeled. You should note the raw material the vinegar was made from, the quantity, the strength,the dates of manufacture, dates of aging, and date of bottling. The location of these events and the makers name also adds a nice touch, especially on decorative bottles.

# CHAPTER 5

## THE PRODUCTION OF VINEGAR STOCK

### CONVERSION OF SUGARS TO ALCOHOL

Vinegar stock, wash and substrate are a few of the names that are given to the alcoholic mixture that will be used to make vinegar. To make a good vinegar, it is necessary to make or obtain a good vinegar stock. As mentioned in the raw materials section, many different materials can be used to make this stock. It is beyond the scope of this book to cover vinegar stock production in depth, but since it is so closely related to the production of vinegar, it warrants a brief discussion. See the appendix for books that cover the subject more thoroughly.

## YEAST TYPES

The conversion of sugars to alcohol is a result of the action of yeasts. The process is anaerobic, which means that it occurs in the absence of air. It is not difficult to create an anaerobic atmosphere because large volumes of carbon dioxide gas are produced that displace the oxygen if the equipment is correctly designed. The process will then proceed anaerobically by itself.

Wild yeasts are present in the air. And though they can be used to convert sugar to alcohol they often produce undesirable tastes and aromas. Pure cultures assure a consistently pleasing product and are preferred for this reason. The type of yeast used depends on the product being turned into alcohol and the desired end taste.

Two yeast species are commonly used in industrial fermentation of sugars to alcohols: *Saccharomyces cerevisiae* or brewer's yeast and *Saccharomyces ellipsoideus*, or wine yeast. *Saccharomyces cerevisiae* var. *diastaticus* is used to convert malt sugars to alcohol. As a rule, Brewer's yeast is preferred where the mash obtained is to be fermented from grains,cereals or molasses. Wine yeast is preferred for fermenting fruit juices and honey.

Many strains of these species of yeast are known. They are kept in pure culture and some of these cultures have been "educated" to use many different materials to produce high alcohol yields or otherwise become specially adapted to the needs of the vinegar maker. The serious vinegar maker should get an authentic strain of the organisms he needs and take every precaution to keep it pure and vigorous.

## USE OF SULPHUR DIOXIDE

It is economically impractical to pasteurize the juices before fermentation to destroy the undesirable organisms, so sulphur dioxide is used to partially sterilize fruit juices that are about to be fermented to alcohol. [73] There are other benefits as well.

(1) The sugars are more completely fermented.

(2) Increase in yield of approximately 1.8 percent in wine spirits

(3) Undesirable yeasts and lactic acid bacteria are destroyed.

(4) The vinegar has a better and cleaner flavor and aroma.

(5) Vinegar made from fermented juices treated in this manner clear more rapidly.

(6) Acetification of sulphured juices proceeds more rapidly.[74]

The best results are obtained when .06 ounces of potassium metabisulphite, also known as campden tablets, is added to each U.S. gallon of juice. This will be about 175 milligrams of sulphur dioxide per liter. The juice/sulphur mixture is allowed to stand for 24 hours and then put into to a clean, sterile fermentation vessel where a pure and actively fermenting yeast culture is added.

It is essential that all of the sulphur dioxide in the juice be removed, otherwise, it may interfere with subsequent fermentation and acetification. This is done by aerating the mixture or adding food grade hydrogen peroxide ($H_2O_2$)

It is also wise to check the finished product for sulphur dioxide because many people are allergic to it and strict laws on the use of sulphur products have been written to protect them. Kits with instructions to test for sulfites are available at wine-making shops.

For the small-scale vinegar maker, sulfiting is unnecessary, provided all precautions are taken to keep the working area exceptionally clean.

## PREPARATION OF THE STARTER

When the sweetened liquid has been placed in the fermenting vessel, it is very important that the fermentation get started as quickly and completely as possible without contamination by harmful organisms. For this reason, special cultures of the desired yeast are prepared before-hand in relatively large volumes if large batches are being produced. This enormous population may be added immediately. If conditions for the desirable organisms are maintained, there is almost no chance of harmful yeasts or bacteria establishing themselves and doing damage.

For small-scale producers, this is not necessary. Rehydration of the yeast culture is often all that is required. But the method is included to give you a broader view of the vinegar manufacturing process.

## HOW TO PREPARE A YEAST STARTER

After selecting the yeast for fermentation, it is isolated and held in pure culture. From this pure culture, one can then prepare a starter. A large amount of starter is needed to inoculate the main mash, which may contain several thousand gallons in a commercial production.

A tube containing about 10 cubic centimeters of sterile wort is inoculated from a pure culture of the desired yeast. After incubation at a temperature of 77 to 80 degrees centigrade- generally the optimum for yeast culture growth- the culture in the tube may be used to inoculate a larger quantity of sterile mash. After incubation, the contents of the larger container may be used to seed a sterile mash of an even larger quantity. Up to this point, the process is ordinarily carried out in the laboratory, using closed containers. From this point on, the mash inoculated is of semi-plant scale size (10-40 gallons) and is located close to the fermenters. Usually a minimum of one more larger mash, (several hundred gallons), is inoculated and allowed to incubate. Then this fermenting mash, or starter, is added to the main mash. The addition of this enormous yeast culture to the mash is sometimes known as "pitching," and the actively fermenting liquor is sometimes called "gyle".[75]

For the best results, the volume of the starter should be approximately one-tenth of the volume of the sugar solution to be fermented [76]

Since the presence of air tends to speed up the reproduction of new yeast cells and one of the main reasons for a starter is to begin fermentation with a large number of the desired yeast cell, aeration is useful in making up a starter. This is because the rate of yeast reproduction is rather sensitive to environmental factors that do not change the rate of fermentation to the same degree.

The aeration is responsible for removing carbon dioxide, which is a waste product that inhibits yeast cell multiplication but increases alcohol production.

Ethyl alcohol affects yeast cell propagation in much the same way. And though special strains of yeast are also "educated" to produce more alcohol than others, naturally brewed liquids do not normally exceed 20 percent alcohol content. Beverages that contain more alcohol than this are often fortified with distilled spirits.

Using this method, a culture may be started from a single cell and used to inoculate thousands of gallons of mash.

## YEAST FOODS

Yeasts do not live by sugar alone. They also need certain mineral-and nitrogen-containing nutrients. The absence of any one of these classes of nutrients may cause the life activities of the organisms to come to a halt. And a short supply will inevitably slow up the fermentation. This problem is solved by the use of yeast nutrients.

## SUGAR CONCENTRATION:

A sugar concentration of 10 percent to 18 percent usually works nicely. Sometimes, however, commercial producers want to produce a concentrated vinegar and then dilute it with water before bottling it. This allows them to use smaller tanks and fermenters to produce a given amount of vinegar. But other factors must also be considered. Producing a very concentrated vinegar requires a high concentration of sugar, and there are many problems encountered when forcing yeasts to completely ferment such solutions into alcohol. The biggest problem is the competition for water between the yeast and the materials in the solution. If the dissolved solids content is too high, the yeast do not have enough water to carry out normal growth and fermentation will be slowed. When the sugar concentration is too high, the resulting alcohol content could also become high enough to poison the yeast, as well as the vinegar bacteria. Consequently, the desired biological processes may proceed very slowly, or even stop altogether. The unfermented sugars left in the mash will then be wasted and will probably cause the vinegar to spoil.

Since very large volumes will have to be carried in the fermenters without the benefit of an increase in the amount of acetic acid produced, the use of an excessively low concentration of sugars is not economic in large scale production. Additionally this vinegar may not be strong enough to satisfy the requirements of the law if the vinegar is intended for sale. More important to the small scale producer or hobbyist is the fact that the final vinegar may not contain enough acetic acid to be of any use, for pickling, for example, or that it may be so low that it is attacked by microorganisms that are slightly tolerant to acetic acid.

It should be clear now why it is absolutely essential that the sugar levels are accurately measured and adjusted at the very beginning of the operation and that fermentation be stopped immediately when all of the sugar has been changed into alcohol. The initial adjustment of the sugar concentration and the course of the fermentation are usually monitored by the use of a hydrometer.

Specific gravity is measured by the hydrometer and readings obtained by floating the hydrometer in the mash. There are several types of hydrometers. The Brix and Balling hydrometers have scales that show percentage of sugar directly. The Baume hydrometer has an arbitrary numerical scale. The reading on this hydrometer merely compares the weight of the substance being tested with the weight of an equal volume of water. This comparison is referred to as specific gravity. Both of these hydrometer scales can be changed into readings on any of the others by using mathematical formulas or consulting precalculated tables.

Since the temperature of the mash being tested determines its weight per gallon, it is important that hydrometer measurements be carried out at the temperature indicated for the instrument, or if this is not possible that appropriate corrections be made. All good hydrometers indicate the correct temperature at which they are to be used, and the vinegar maker will need to use a reliable thermometer to make such tests accurately.

## TEMPERATURE

It is impossible to recommend the most advantageous temperature for conducting the alcoholic fermentation. This is because so many different sugar solutions are used in vinegar making and also because yeast strains vary in their reactions to various temperatures and temperature change. However, alcoholic fermentations for vinegar making are generally carried out at temperatures ranging from 68 degrees to 85 degrees F..

As mentioned earlier, the yeast species *Saccharomyces cerevisiae*, is recommended for the fermentation of mashes prepared from grains and most sugar solutions, while *Saccharomyces ellipsoideus* is generally preferred to ferment fruit juice. The former species is not as susceptible to small changes in temperature as the latter. Another consideration is the previous history of the culture or strain used. Yeast cultures are living organisms and adapt their behavior to the conditions under which they have been grown for the immediately preceding generations. So when selecting a yeast culture, it is very important to find out from the supplier what the best conditions for growth are, and then follow the directions closely as long as it yields the desired results. If you are not sure of the conditions, you must determine them by experimentation.

Alcohol starts to vaporize at temperatures above 95 degrees F. and serious losses of alcohol may occur if the mash temperature is allowed to rise above this. It must also be remembered that, for the yeast, the alcohol produced is a waste product and is therefore poisonous to it. This means that the alcohol will eventually stop active fermentation if the supply of sugar holds out. At a temperature of 97 degrees F., alcoholic fermentation with an ordinary strain of *Saccharomyces cerevisiae* will stop if the alcohol concentration becomes 3.8 percent. At a temperature of 71 degrees F., the yeast will tolerate 7.3 percent alcohol; at 64.5 degrees F., fermentation will continue until the alcohol content reaches 8.8 percent and at 48 degrees F., fermentation does not stop until a concentration of 9.5 percent is reached. [77] It should be clear from these figures that high concentrations of alcohol are best obtained from the use of this species by low fermentation temperatures. But these low temperatures also lower the speed of fermentation, so a compromise has to be reached.

This means that some thought should be given to the question of temperature control when designing a new vinegar facility beyond the hobbyist level. Two factors that will often raise the temperature of the alcohol fermenter are weather, and the conversion of sugars into alcohol, which is an exothermic reaction (When a chemical change gives off heat it is an exothermic reaction, for example, the burning of paper). If it is cold, the temperature of the fermenting mash may be unnecessarily lowered to a point where the process may be too slow or the fermentation may stop altogether. To manage these problems there should be a way to warm or cool the fermenter. This is done by inserting a heating or cooling coil directly into the mash or installing a temperature-controlled ventilation system into the room. Although not really necessary, equipment like this is available even for the small-scale hobbyist.

## PRIMARY AND SECONDARY FERMENTATION

Ordinarily, if conditions are right, the yeast fermentation will take place in two rather clearly defined stages. First there is a period of primary fermentation when most of the sugar is converted into carbon dioxide and alcohol. During this stage the process is so active that foreign organisms find it hard to develop in numbers great enough to cause a problem. This primary fermentation is generally finished within three to six days.

Then the secondary fermentation occurs which usually takes from two to three weeks. This is the time when the danger of contamination by undesirable organisms is greatest. The Mycoderma yeasts, sometimes called "wine flowers", and the lactic acid bacteria present special problems for the vinegar maker and you must be careful to keep them out of the process

If the hydrometer readings show that the secondary fermentation is very slow, the fermenting liquid can be aerated to reactivate the yeast. During this period the temperatures should also be watched closely because the secondary fermentation is more vulnerable to cold than the primary stage. If this happens, the solution of course, is to artificially raise the temperature to a more favorable level.

## SETTLING AND RACKING

After the fermentation has stopped, the solids like the yeast and fruit pulp, tend to settle rapidly into a compact sediment at the bottom of the fermentation vessel. The fermented liquid must be separated from this sediment as soon and as completely as possible. The sediment is rich in nitrogenous materials which are very likely to rot and introduce unwanted flavors which will end up in the completed vinegar.

This separation process is commonly referred to as "racking". It is usually done by.pumping or syphoning off the clear liquid.

The remaining sediment will contain a lot of of alcoholic liquid which could be used for vinegar stock, but the amount of filtration necessary to isolate it from the contaminating solids is generally not worth the bother. So it is better to use this sediment to make more of the same type of alcohol if it can be kept pure or just discard it.

## STORAGE OF THE VINEGAR STOCK

The vinegar stock should have a specific gravity or Balling hydrometer reading of near 0. In other words, there should be no sugar. When it has reached this point, one of two procedures should be followed. The vinegar stock should be stored in completely filled and sealed vessels to exclude air. This will prevent the growth of unwanted aerobic (air-loving) organisms that will cause trouble if allowed to grow. The other option is to store the vinegar stock in open vessels. In this case, vinegar should be added until it contains at least 1 percent acetic acid. The first method is the preferred method and is rather easy for the hobbyist to accomplish. In addition to providing the most protection from things getting in, it also keeps the alcohol and important volatile oils from getting out.

## WINE MAKING MADE TOO SIMPLE
### BUT IT WORKS

| | | |
|---|---|---|
| NECKED CONTAINER<br>AIR LOCK<br>YEAST      FILTER<br>ANY NATURAL JUICE<br>FUNNEL | | |
| **ASSEMBLE THESE ITEMS** | **FILL CONTAINER HALF FULL WITH THE JUICE** | **ADD WINE YEAST** |
| | | ROOM TEMP<br>ROOM |
| **FILL AIR LOCK WITH WATER** | **PLACE AIR LOCK ASSEMBLY INTO MOUTH OF CONTAINER** | **PLACE THE WHOLE SET UP IN A WARM BUT CONVINIENT PLACE. LEAVE FOR 2 WEEKS** |
| **CHECK** | | |
| **WATCH FOR FOAMING WITHIN 2 DAYS. IF FOAM ENTERS AIR LOCK, CLEAN AND REPLACE** | **CHECK TASTE. IF STILL SWEET LEAVE UNTIL NO SUGAR CAN BE TASTED. +- A 3 DAYS** | **FILTER OR SIPHON OFF THE WINE. IT IS NOW READY FOR VINEGAR MAKING !** |

This is just to give you the basic idea of how wine is made. The ancients, however, made millions of gallons of wine with a lot less trouble than this. Unless you are lucky, the results will not be consistent or great, but it will give you the experience you will need to get better without a large expenditure of time or money. And, anyway, you are going to refine it into vinegar.

Remember to keep every thing clean.

Check health food stores and the juice rack at large supermarkets for juices that are very tasty and have a high enough sugar content to give you a wine strong enough to make a good vinegar. Make sure that they are natural juices, not juice drinks or other "fake juice" products. Also be sure that no sugar or preservatives have been added. Sometimes the sugar content as well as other useful information is listed right on the bottle. Clear juices often contain sulphites to keep them from turning brown, so check the label carefully.

Try to get a good yeast. A champagne yeast generally gives a dry wine, which is best for vinegar making. If you cannot get this, try bread yeast. But don't count on great results. Wine hobby shops personel can help you find a suitable yeast if you are not familiar with this.

# CHAPTER 6

## MAKING VINEGAR

### ALCOHOL TO ACETIC ACID CONVERSION

Much of the vinegar made in the United States is made by the submerged process in Frings acetators. This process will be discussed in more detail later. But the method is impractical for most people because of the high capital outlay and the technical skills necessary to start and keep the system in operation. Anyway, what would you do with more than 30,000 gallons of vinegar per day.

The highest qualities of vinegar are developed in the slow process. The hobbyist cannot compete with the manufacturers who mass produce vinegar in terms of quantity. But because hobbyist production runs are very small, he can afford to experiment. This means he can compete very well when it comes to quality.

It is assumed at this point that you have read all of the material in the production section up to this point. If you haven't, keep that fact in mind and refer back to that material or the troubleshooting chapter should you have problems.

Whenever possible, assemble everything you need before beginning. It will make the making of vinegar a lot simpler and more enjoyable.

## HOME METHODS OF PRODUCTION

It is best to start the vinegar-making process with a vinegar stock (alcoholic wash) of 9 percent. This will generally yield a vinegar content of about 7.5 percent acetic acid. Note that this is a much stronger vinegar than is normally used or needed, so water can be added to dilute it to a more useful concentration. If pickling, however, this concentration can sometimes be useful. A vinegar stock of 6 percent will yield a vinegar of 4.6 percent to 4.8 percent in acid strength. This wash may be from fruit or from grain.

Several different ways will be given to make vinegar. However, we will start out with a method that will include all of the basic principals for making vinegar. Once you have become familiar with this method you may want to invest in more and better materials and equipment to make better vinegars.

First, you will need two containers, one for making the vinegar and another for storing it. Other containers for racking, etc. will also be useful. If you are fortunate enough to find a container in which vinegar has be previously made, grab it! This will, under normal circumstances, greatly increase your chances of success. Otherwise use glass or unleaded ceramics and save yourself a lot of headaches.

To maintain an optimum temperature, the generating container should be kept in the house or other convenient place where the ambient temperature is reasonably warm. Electric heating coils are also available that can be inserted directly into the brewing vinegar if temperature control is a problem. The storage container should always be kept in the cellar or some other cool dark place.

Both containers should have been selected using all of the principals previously outlined (see utensils). Additionally, the generating container should be selected and arranged so as to provide as much surface area for the fermenting vinegar as possible. A wooden barrel or ceramic crock should work fine. This will help to make large amounts of air available to the bacteria.

Conversely, the storage container should have almost no surface area. A glass, ceramic or baked enamel container with a small neck and mouth is the best choice here. A glass jug with a small neck can be made to serve both purposes(see graphics). This will stop the acetification oxidation process. If this is not done, the acetobacters may convert your vinegar into carbon dioxide and water. Proper storage containers also help to keep unwanted organisms out and flavor and aroma in.

Fill the generating container to about one-third of its capacity with your selected vinegar stock.

Then add a live vinegar starter culture until the container is half full.

Set this container in a warm place (75 degrees to 86 degrees F.).

Test it about once every three days.

Keep records

## LOG BOOK

When it approaches the desired or maximum strength, test once every other day.

Let it remain in the generator until it has reached its desired or maximum strength.

Rack it of into the aging container and add woods if desired.

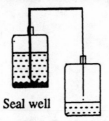

Seal well

Store in cool place.

After aging is finished, rack off and/or clarify if desired.

If desired bottle and label.

Don't forget to log everything

# ORLEANS PROCESS

The Orleans method is the oldest-known commercial process of making vinegar. It is still in use today, and is still considered one of the best ways to produce high-quality vinegars. It is named after the French city where a vinegar industry that was famous for the quality of its product was established many generations ago.

If you want to make vinegar in much larger quantities and still turn out a high-quality product, it is suggested that you use the Orleans method.

You will need a barrel of about 50-gallons to make a convertor or generator.

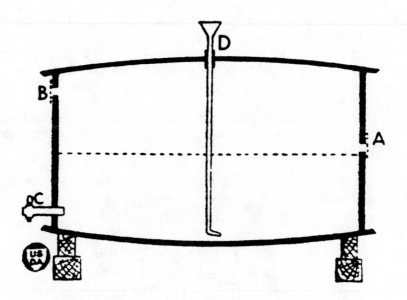

## CONVERTER FOR CONTINUOUS ORLEANS PROCESS

1. In one end of the barrel you make a 2 inch hole (A).

2. At the other end of the barrel, you make another hole about the same size (B).

3. The holes are covered with netting or well-varnished wire screen to keep out vinegar flies.

4. A spigot is fitted in place (See C)

5. Using a hot iron, put a hole in the cork that will go into the bung hole (See C for cork and D for bung hole).

6. Put a glass or plastic funnel about halfway through the hole in the cork.

7. A piece of bent glass tubing about one half-inch in diameter, and just long enough to reach to within three inches of the bottom of the barrel is then fitted into the other end of the half (see diagram Fig.2)

8. The fitted converter is then firmly secured in a place where there is plenty of free circulating air.

9. About three gallons of fresh unpasteurized vinegar is poured into the barrel.

10. The vinegar stock of about 9 percent alcohol is then added to the barrel until the surface of the liquid is nearly level with the air hole (see A)

10. If the vinegar stock is warmed slightly, not above 90 degrees F., The process will start faster. But this is not absolutely necessary.

11.The converter is then allowed to stand until the acetic acid concentration reaches the desired level.

# TRANSFERRING THE VINEGAR

## RACKING OFF

Transfer of the vinegar should be done very slowly so as not to disturb or break the mother. It is quite likely that a mother of vinegar will form on the surface of this liquid. Some makers throw the contents of the barrel out and start over. Others prize this mother and take it as a sign that all is going well. Suit yourself. There are reasonable arguments for both points of view. If you are going to save the mother, it must not be disturbed. If it falls to the bottom it could ruin your vinegar.

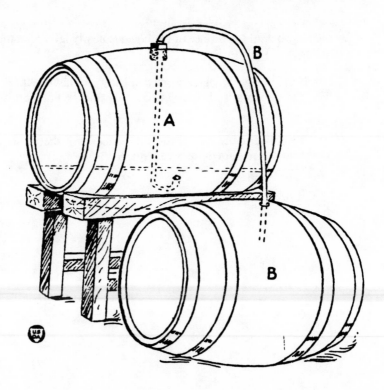

1. Draw off the vinegar until you have about three gallons left.in your 50-gallon barrel.

2. More vinegar stock is then slowly added through the funnel that leads to the bottom of the converter. This should also be done very slowly so as not to disturb the mother, which should rise as the barrel is filled. The fermentation process will start all over again.

From this point, you can proceed to finish your vinegar. A converter of this type should convert about 100 to 150 gallons of 9 percent alcohol into vinegar per year. Don't forget to log everything.

## RICE VINEGAR

Rice vinegar has long been the vinegar of choice in the Orient. It can be processed using high-tech systems that greatly speed up the process. But there are great advantages to making it the "old way." Like the great balsamics, there is some controversy about just exactly how it is done, so don't be surprised if someone tells you it should not be done this way. If you meet someone who says they know a better way and they are making it themselves, try their system. Over time you will develop your own. This may not be the best way, but it works, and it will get you started.

Polished rice is placed in a container and soaked in water for about 12 to 15 hours. When the rice is saturated with water, it is steamed (**not boiled**) for about one hour and 20 minutes or until the core of the grains are cooked. The steamed rice is then taken out of the steamer and cooled.

It is then put into clean containers. At this point, either the mold *Aspergillus oryzae* or an enzyme extract is added to the rice to convert its starch into sugar.

Instructions for the using the enzyme comes with it. Unless you are familiar with "Koji," as the mold is called in Japanese, it is best to use the enzyme. There is a much greater chance for success with a lot less time, money and hassle.

When the starch has been converted into sugar, you will have a mush of sweet rice in a broth. Strain the liquid from the rice. Now test it to see how completely the starch has been converted to sugar.

Check for the presence of starch with an iodine test. Check the sugar content with a hydrometer. If the sugar content is too low, some people add sugar to bring it up to the desired level. A purist would never do this, and if the starch is fully converted you will not need to either.

Now add the yeast and proceed as you would if you were using wine.

After you have an alcoholic mash, you can follow the home method.

## *NEW*

It is now possible to purchase rice sugar which has been made directly from rice. Using this product will simplify the making rice vinegar considerably. Check with the suppliers of home brewing materials for supplies and instruction on using it..

## SAKE VINEGAR

The purists distinguish vinegar made from rice and vinegar made from sake. If you want to make a rice-based vinegar from sake, use the following method.

Choose a sake that has a good aroma and taste. Then convert it using the "home" method for making vinegar. Make sure to

check the alcohol and sulphite levels. When there is failure ,
these are the likely culprits.

## PASTEUR PROCESS

Louis Pasteur, the great French microbiologist, was the first to
understand the need for keeping large quantities of air available
to the fermenting vinegar. He used a wooden raft on which the
mother could grow. This addition allowed more air to come in
contact with the vinegar and while preventing the mother from
falling to improve the production rates.

## OTHER SMALL-SCALE SYSTEMS

Many other systems have been devised which produce vinegar,
but all of them operate on the same basic principles as those just
described.

## COMMERCIAL PROCESSES

Commercial processes are more complicated than home
methods. They are designed to increase the yields of vinegar.
The exact procedure requires a lot more detail than can be laid
out here, but a good overview is given to help you further
understand and appreciate the world of vinegar.

## QUICK OR RAPID GENERATORS

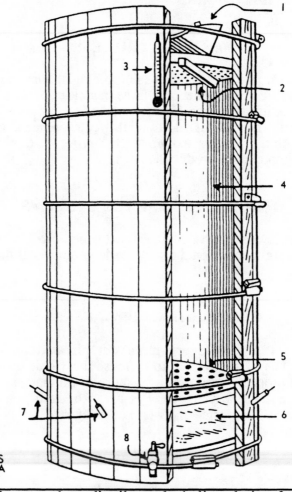

1-Tipping trough to distribute alcoholic solution from which vinegar is to be made: 2-distributing head; 3-thermometer; 4-acetification compartment to be filled with packing material; 5-false bottom; 6-vinegar collection compartment; 7-ports for regulating incoming air; 8- spigot for letting vinegar out.

Vinegar generators are made in various sizes and shapes (see diagram). They are usually made of narrow strips of wood, which may be cypress, fir, oak or redwood. They are held together by iron hoops that are fitted with draw lugs. They are about twice as high as they are round and have false bottoms with holes through which air is allowed or forced to enter. This air then passes over the porous material with which the generator is packed.

Any materials that have large surface areas may be used if they do not contain materials that are soluble in the liquid or that will leech out and ruin the flavor of the vinegar.

Some materials have natural or economic advantages over others. Wood charcoal is not as durable as charcoal. Corn cobs are not particularly durable, but they are often cheap and easy to find in certain areas. But whatever material is used in the generator, it should be soaked and rinsed thoroughly with water and then with vinegar before it is used.

If the generator is very large, another perforated shelf is usually installed about halfway between the top and bottom of the tank. This shelf helps to support this porous material. A device for introducing the vinegar stock is generally installed near the top of the generator and above the porous material to permit even distribution over the top surface of the packing material. This may be a rotating sprinkler or sparger, or an automatic feed trough[78].

The vinegar stock may be passed repeatedly through the same generator until it has reached the desired acidity, or it may be passed through two or three sets of generators in series, increasing in acidity with each pass. A generator 10 feet in diameter and 20 feet high can be expected to produce between 80 and 100 U.S. gallons of vinegar per day[79] (see section 1 for historical information).

## THE FRINGS ACETATOR

The Frings acetator is the state of the art when it comes to vinegar production. Like all other quick processes, it can not compete with the Orleans method for quality. But it more than makes up for this deficit in quantity. Since the process is rather secret, there are few materials that explain it in much understandable detail. To find out how it works it was necessary to talk to someone who works with it on a day to day basis. Scott Zuniga is the operations manager of American Foods in Cucamonga, California, and he explained his operation .

"The acetator is basically a large stainless-steel vessel with various types of baffles inside the unit to control the foaming. You have a series of cooling coils, you have an impeller at the bottom, you have inlets for air and you have various external control pumps and things to control the process.

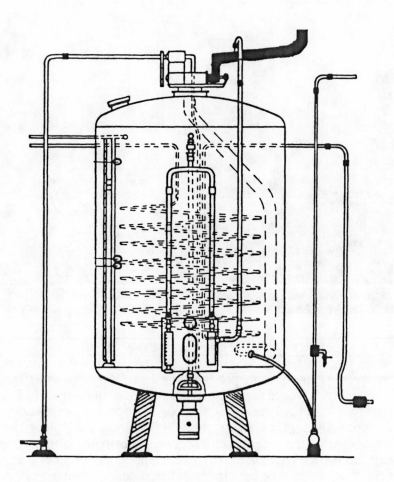

## DIAGRAM OF FRINGS ACETATOR

"Basically you have alcohol, a starter culture from a previous batch and you have nutrients for the product. You maintain constant monitoring of the alcohol and the acetic acid contents.

As it gradually converts, the acetobacters increase in population. As the production continues the bacteria populations increase.

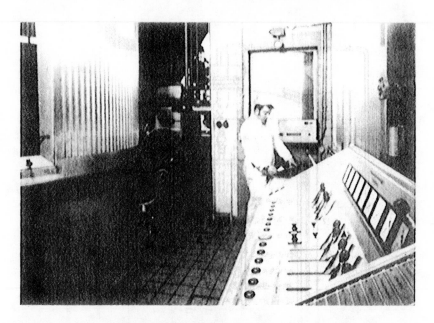

CONTROL PANEL FOR VINEGAR PLANT

"Also there is heat developed during the process that must be removed. The bacteria produce the heat. Any fermentation, whether its a yeast fermentation or a bacterial fermentation, produces heat, the heat of respiration. The optimum temperature is about 88 degrees F. to about 95 degrees F. Below that temperature, the acetobacter become dormant; above that temperature the bacteria die off and you no longer produce acetic acid. You remove the heat by an external heat exchange system. We happen to use a cooling tower in which we circulate cold water that is subsequently cooled by evaporation.

"We bring air from the atmosphere. We maintain very tight controls over the gradual conversion process, checking about every three hours. And when the product reaches 12 to 13 percent acetic acid level and a .5 percent residual alcohol in about 36 to 48 hours, 40 to 50 percent of it is removed. The remainder is left as a starter culture. The acetator is refilled with new stock and the process begins all over again.

"It is referred to as a submerged fermentation process. You are creating a product that is maintained under a highly aerobic condition by very carefully controlling temperature, air injection and volume. You must also control the foaming and bacterial populations. By doing this you gradually turn the alcohol substrate into vinegar."

This process, with occasionally some slight variation, is used by the majority of the high-volume vinegar producers. There are reports that Japanese have recently improved this technique, but their technology is not for sale.

## IMMOBILIZED CELL PRODUCTION

Recently, other processes of vinegar production using immobilized acetobacters have been developed. Hydrous titanium IV oxide, ceramic monolith, polypropylene fibers, cotton like propylene and K-carrageenan gel have been used as carriers. Though each of these processes rapidly produced acetic acid, the acid produced was of lower acidity than conventional generators. Their rates of production are also too hypersensitive to oxygen deficits to be of commercial use. For that reason, they are merely laboratory curiosities at this time.[80]

## MALT VINEGAR PRODUCTION

We find some of the best malt vinegars in the world produced in England. The name alegar is more correct, but this term is not used as much as it should be. Commercial production is carried out using a tower fermentator

The process begins with the delivery of bulk grain to silos where it is cleaned and destoned by a vibrating screen. It is weighed before being steeped in water. The wet grain is then crushed. Following this, it is transported by means of a large screwing device into a cooking vessel where water and "weak returns" are added. Weak returns are solutions that are left over from the previous spargings. The soaking and cooking are continued in one of the two mash vessels under strict temperature control.

The resulting liquid is called a wort. A vessel called a Lauter Tun separates the spent grain from the wort. The spent grain is used for cattle fodder. The wort is collected in a measuring vessel and more weak returns are added until a 15 Balling sugar concentration is produced. Surplus weaks from this operation are saved for the next batch.

The sweet wort is pasteurized through a plate heat exchanger and fed into tower fermentators at the rate of 250 gallons per hour. During the passage through the tower the wort is converted into a 5.5 percent alcoholic wort. The carbon dioxide that is generated from the process is vented into the atmosphere.

The wort overflows to a header tank controlled with level switches that control the tank discharge. Then a secondary fermentation is carried out in large holding vats where the alcohol level is increased to 6 percent.

After the secondary fermentation, the wort is passed to holding vats.

The acetification system is made up of four aerated vessels of about 9,000 gallons each that contain cooling coils. The aeration is accomplished by blowing air through a series of porous plastic tubes. The batch of wort is initially primed with acetobacter that convert the alcohol into acetic acid. About one-third of this is drained and released every 24 hours.

**MALT VINEGAR PLANT**

The raw vinegar is then diluted and stored or used right away for sauce manufacturing. When it is to be bottled for consumer use-the raw vinegar is clarified by passing it through a bed of beechwood chips. This process takes between three and six months

It is then filtered through a membrane, and other ingredients such as caramel and water are added before pasteurization and bottling.

All grains including rice and corn can be processed using similar systems.

## VINEGAR PRODUCTION FLOW CHART

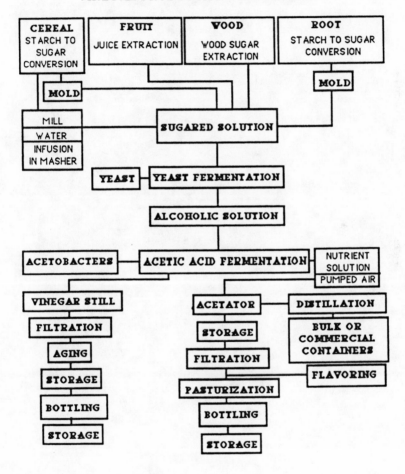

# CHAPTER 7

## POST PRODUCTION VINEGARS

After vinegar has been made, it can be further altered. The alteration of vinegar constitutes an art in and of itself. Aging, flavoring, scenting and blending are used. Aging has already been discussed.

## FLAVORING VINEGARS

Vinegars may be flavored with many different materials. Although woods are the most common and are responsible for the great taste of the finest vinegars, various other plants may be used. It is possible to use herbs, spices, fruits or vegetables. Combinations of these may also be employed. These taste can also be changed depending on which vinegar is used. (see flavoring materials appendix for list of suggestions).

Choose the vinegar well. Vinegars that are sharp or harsh will probably remain that way, overpowering the subtle taste of the flavoring materials. Those that have poor taste probably will not be improved with the addition of precious materials.

There are two basic ways to flavor vinegar: a cold process and a hot process. The process used largely depends on the material used for flavoring.

The cold process is preferred for substances with delicate flavors and aromas because more of their subtle qualities are preserved with this method. In this case, the flavoring material is added to the vinegar and left until the vinegar is sufficiently flavored. It is generally best to place the container in a sunny window. If this is not possible, the room temperature should always be at least 70 degrees, preferably higher.

When the vinegar is sufficiently flavored, the flavoring agent is removed, usually by straining, and the flavoring agent discarded. The vinegar is then bottled, corked and sealed with wax. It is stored in a cool, dark place for about six months before use. It can be used right away, but the aromas tend to blend better with time.

There are notable exceptions such as saffron. The saffron fragrance will be very dominate for a few weeks and then tends to deteriorate after a while. Materials such as these should be made in very small quantities and used right away for best results.

In the hot process, the materials are processed as though they were tea. The vinegar is heated and either poured over the materials or the materials are placed into the vinegar at just below boiling temperature. The flavoring material is strained out and discarded, and the vinegar is stored in a cool, dark place for about six months before use to improve the flavor.

As a rule, the greater the surface area, the better the diffusion rate into the vinegar. For this reason the materials are bruised, cut or crushed before being used. The amount of flavor-contributing substances contained in the material will vary from season to season, so individual judgment must dictate how much you use. Recipes are given in the Vinegar Flavoring Materials appendix.

Make sure the utensils used conform to the guidelines offered under UTENSILS. Heating the vinegar makes the reaction with the improper materials more pronounced.

## SCENTING VINEGARS

Scented vinegars can be used as a room freshener, a body or hair rinse and in any other case where where a fresh, clean scent is needed (see uses section). Since vinegar is quite volatile, it will evaporate quite readily. When it does, it will take with it the aromas of the substances it is scented with.

Scenting is best carried out with the cold process used for flavoring because fewer of the volatile oils evaporate during processing.

## BLENDING VINEGARS

Blending is another way to enjoy working with vinegar. By acquiring vinegars from various sources, it is possible to mix them together and obtain rather unique blends. This is done to alter the taste, acetic acid levels or appearance.

The important consideration, other than taste is acetic acid level. On a commercial, level it is important to stay above the 4.5 percent acetic acid level. For the hobbyist, it is not critical. In fact, he may deliberately lower the strength of the vinegar for salad dressings or beverages. However if the vinegar is to be used for pickling it should be at least 4.5 percent because the vinegar will pull water from the pickled material and lower the acid level considerably. If the acid level is too low, the preservative effect will be lost. Learning to titrate acid strength accurately will be worth the time and effort for those interested in this aspect of the art.

What is needed is a familiarity with those vinegars already produced and an objective of the new taste you desire. Small quantities may be taste tested until you have found just the right combination in just the right amounts.

Then you are ready to move onto the next step. Determine the total volume of the blended vinegar desired, then mix the vinegars in that proportion to give you that total volume.

---

### EXAMPLE

You have determined that the perfect blend for this vinegar will be;

        2 parts of vinegar A
        3 parts of vinegar B
        5 parts of vinegar C

You have decided that you want to make ten gallons of this blend. So you mix

        2 gallons of vinegar A
        3 gallons of vinegar B
        <u>5 gallons of vinegar C</u>
        10 gallons of the new blend

---

Record keeping is very important. It is very frustrating to come up with a great blend only to be unable to reproduce it. Gathering as much information as possible about the vinegars that go into your blend is also important. This information is not always available, but the more you know about vinegars the fewer "secrets" there will be. Like a wine connoisseur, as a vinegar connoisseur you will be able to tell a lot about the vinegars just from their appearance, aroma and taste.

# CHAPTER 8

## TROUBLE SHOOTING

### Success is built on failure[81].

No doubt you will run into some problems making vinegar. But remember "there are only so many ways to do something wrong, so if you keep on trying, you will eventually run out of wrong ways and will be left with only the right way to do it."[82]

## OVEROXIDATION

The chief cause of failure in making vinegar is over oxidation by the acetobacters. This problem can be reduced by cutting off the supply of air to the vinegar at the appropriate time before all of the all of the alcohol is turned into vinegar. Pasteurization and filtration will also help if air and new acetobacters are excluded from the vinegar after these processes are completed.

## VINEGAR MOLD

Vinegar is also destroyed by the mold *Moniliella acetoabutans* [83]. Adding the right amount of vinegar to the starting culture and maintaining a clean environment will greatly decrease the chance for the organism to get established. If it does get established, sterilize everything and start over.

## ANTIBIOTICS

If your vinegar culture does not convert the alcohol or stops after the addition of new alcohol, you may have added an antibiotic such as sulfites or sorbates. Some of the wines you use to make your vinegar may contain ascorbic acid, potassium sorbate or sulphur products like potassium metabisulfate, sodium metabisulfite or sulphur dioxide gas, which turns into sulphur dioxide in solution. These products are used to keep the wines from being destroyed by microorganisms. This means their purpose is to interfere with any fermentation process, including vinegar fermentation.

With sorbates very little can be done so check the labels beforehand, and in the case of large quantities have it tested by a competent lab. Over a long period of time it will decompose. It can also be diluted to a non-toxic level by blending it with other alcohols which are known to contained no sorbates.

There are two methods to get rid of sulfites. They can be aerated by passing air bubbles through them or letting the affected vinegar stock stand for a few months. The use of the devices used to aerate fish tanks work very well for the hobby-level vinegar producer. Be sure to monitor the acid levels in case this aeration starts to increase your rate of vinegar production. This will only remove the "free" sulphur dioxide but will generally work well enough to produce a good vinegar.

All of the sulphites can be removed by adding food-grade hydrogen peroxide. This will instantly inactivate the sulfiting agents. The right amount must be added so that the hydrogen peroxide is also used up in the reaction. For example, 1 ml of 3 percent solution of hydrogen peroxide will remove 10 parts per million of $SO_2$ per gallon of wine.

## SINGLE STEP FERMENTATION

Another cause of failure is the attempt at making the vinegar in a single process. Remember, it is a double- or triple-fermentation process and every effort should be made to keep these processes separate. This almost always requires separate containers for each fermentation process.

## TEMPERATURE

Fermenting at a temperature that is too low or too high can cause many problems. Always monitor, adjust and record temperatures as often as practically possible (see temperature).

## STRANGE COLOR OR APPEARANCE

The vinegar may turn dark. Often, this is a natural process and should not cause alarm. However, if the vinegar turns extremely black, then it is very likely that you have somehow contaminated the vinegar with iron. Iron will combine with the tannins in the vinegar to give the vinegar an inky color. The best solution for this batch of vinegar is to discard it and start over again.

## VINEGAR FLIES

> One catches more flies with a spoonful of vinegar than with 20 casks of vinegar.
> Henry V of France[84]

Good old Henry must have never visited a vinegar plant or never heard of the vinegar fly. Because wherever there is vinegar, you are certain to find the vinegar fly, also known as fruit fly, also known as *Drosophila* sub species (see electron micrographs by Deborah Clayton).

These tiny flies have the uncanny ability to find fruit and fruit by-products, like vinegar, miles into the desert, deep in caves and high on mountains. Certainly, they will have no trouble finding your vinegar.

Fortunately they don't eat much If the larvae of these flies get into your vinegar it could deteriorate the vinegar.Aside from this, they are little more that  an aesthetic nuisance.

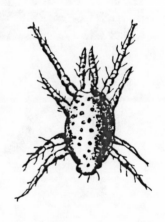

The quantity of the flies may be greatly decreased by keeping the place screened and spotlessly clean, avoiding vinegar spills and cleaning up any spills and leaks immediately. You are reminded that all of the openings to the vinegar still must be well screened to keep out any vinegar flies.

## VINEGAR MITES

Unless your production space is very clean, you may eventually attract vinegar mites (*Tyroglyphus longior L , Tyroglyphus firo Gerv*) Under just the right conditions of warmth and moisture, these mites will breed rather rapidly. And unless proper precautions are taken they will get into the vinegar and spoil it. These mites are readily destroyed with hot water or steam. If the infestation is really bad, the whole room should be fumigated with sulphur. But keep in mind that sulphur is also unwanted in the processing of vinegar and so care should be taken to eliminate it before starting your production again.

Vinegar Mite (*Bersch*).

## VINEGAR EELS

Vinegar eels (also known as *Anguillula aceti* or *Turbotrix aceti*), are very small, 1/16 of an inch long, worms or nematodes which often find their way into vinegar production. Although these nematodes are very small, they can be seen by the naked eye by holding a small glass of them up to a strong light. These eels are harmless if swallowed, but they don't add much to the aesthetics of the finished product.

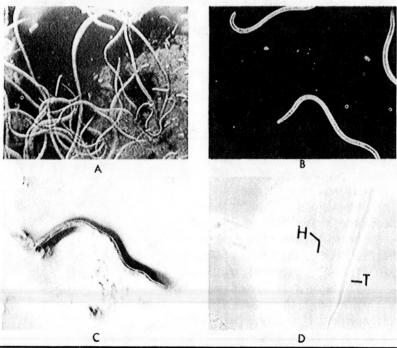

A. As they appear magnified in vinegar. B. Singled out. C. 3-D effect photo allowing visualization of the surface of the eel. D. H= head, T= tail looking through the membrane of the V. eel.

There is quite a bit of controversy as to the role the vinegar eel plays in the production of vinegar. Generally, they are considered undesirable. Balsamic producers live in fear of them, because their extremely valuable product will be significantly devalued by the infestation of these animals.

Pasteur thought they diminished the quality of the vinegar. However, recent studies have found that many industrial vinegar generators that are infested with vinegar eels show no apparent detriment to the operation. In fact, they found that there was actually a higher production of acetic acid and greater efficiencies of conversion in those generators that contained the eels. It is thought that the vinegar eels act as scavengers, keeping the generator free of dead acetobacters.[85]

These eels are very easily removed from the vinegar by pasteurization and filtration. Any barrels, tanks, generators or any other containers where the eels are found can be cleaned with steam.

## HEAVY METALS

If heavy metal levels are too high, they can inhibit acid production. Sometimes these are found naturally in the fruits, like apples that often pick up high levels of lead, copper, arsenic and iron from the soil. Other times they may be from the water or equipment. The small-scale operation is not likely to be seriously bothered by this problem. If it does become a problem, then the source should be identified and removed.

## POWER FAILURES

In large-scale vinegar production power failure is a major threat. When this happens, all of the pumps stop running, the cooling system shuts down, and the impellers quit. And since you need to maintain a high concentration of air for the artificially crowded bacteria to survive at this rapid rate of production, in order to get higher acid strength (12 percent), a shut down of about 30 seconds will essentially kill the culture. It will take a week to 10 days for the acetator to regain its working culture again.

To be ready to deal with this problem, it is necessary to keep an electrical generator on standby at all times.

## FOAMING

Foaming presents another problem to commercial producers who use methods that employ high rates of forced aeration. They have controlled this problem with new equipment designs and anti-foaming agents. But the anti-foaming agents have fallen out of favor because they increase the air bubble size which reduces the rate at which oxygen transfers to the vinegar.

## FALLING MOTHERS

In the slow processes, the mother of vinegar sometimes falls. If the mother starts to rot, it can impart an off taste to the vinegar. What is likely to be an even bigger problem is the accumulation of mother to the point that there is more mother than vinegar. A vinegar still can literally be filled with the cellulose material that the mother is made of.

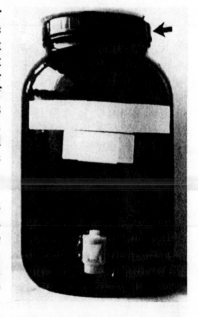

There are a number of solutions to these problems. One is to use a container that allows you to remove the mother by hand. Wash and rinse you hands well before sticking them in the vinegar.

Another is to make a wooden raft for the mother to float on. (see Pasture process). Sometimes a change of temperature will slow the production of mother and sometimes the addition of another type of alcohol substrate will work. Periodic aeration with a fish tank type aerator will sometimes inhibit the formation of mother. Regular aeration may stop mothering, but it may also speed up the slow process too much. This increased speed may deteriorate the vinegar's quality and may create acid-level monitoring problems for the amateur.

# CHAPTER 9

## BALSAMIC VINEGAR

Balsamic vinegar is also known as Aceto Balsamico, Aceto Balsamico di Modena and Aceto del Duca.[86] Balsamico in Italian means balm or aromatic. Balm means a healing or soothing medicine. Aromatic means a medicinal substance with a spicy fragrance and stimulant qualities.[87] So it is clear from the name that balsamic vinegar has the reputation of having medicinal qualities. It is also reported to be an aphrodisiac. It was used as a gargle, tonic and air purifier against the plague in the 17th century. As a result, it became a custom to travel with a supply of the vinegar in a small barrel fitted with handles as a precautionary measure.[88]

For many years its manufacture and use were rather restricted to Italy. It was unknown to those living outside of the region where it is made. World-famous cooking encyclopedias like the *Larousse Gastronomique* do not even mention it. However, it has now spread to shops and supermarkets throughout Europe and even to the United States. But it is in Modena where the vinegar is appreciated most. Specially trained tasters, the Maestri Assagiatori must pass rigorous test of competence under the aegis of the Consorteria dell' Aceto Balsamico Naturale Spilamberto. This is an exclusive and fraternal organization whose members are bound by their strong love of balsamic vinegar.

TOWN OF MODENA

In Modena, Balsamic vinegar is not just vinegar, it is a symbol of sophistication, a good investment, and a way of life.

The prices range from a few dollars per bottle (this is rarely if ever the genuine article) to more than $300 for a 7 1/2 ounce bottle from a batteria dated 1730. This makes the vinegar one of the most expensive condiments in the world and equal in investment value to many precious metals.

In Italy, it is so highly prized that sometimes it is not sold at all. It is saved by the family for special gifts or dowries. The very best balsamics may be reserved for close associates and family. It is also occasionally used to reward a special service rendered. Boniface, Marquis of Bologna and Modena made a gift of balsamic vinegar to Henry III, The Holy Roman Emperor in 1046 AD. The dukes of Modena continued the tradition of making gifts of this precious vinegar until the territories were dissolved in the 19th century.

There are two kinds of balsamic vinegar: the natural or real (Aceto Balsamico naturale) and the industrial or imitation (Aceto Balsamico industriale).The industrial version, though often pleasing to taste, and usually superior to many other commercial vinegars, shares only a name with the natural product. The industrial version of the product is nothing more than boiled down trebbiano grapes that have been mixed with regular vinegar,flavored and colored with caramelized sugar, herbs and other ingredients. It is aged as little as one year. It is then purified and sold as a kind of standard household vinegar around the area of Modena. Outside of Modena, where most people cannot distinguish the difference, it is sometimes sold as real balsamic vinegar at about the same price as good wine.

According to the master tasters of Consorteria dell' Aceto Balsamico, in Spilamberto Italy, "Genuine, natural Aceto Balsamico is produced in the area of the states of the former Este family. It is produced from boiled down grape juice, matured by slow acetification produced by natural alcoholic fermentation and progressively concentrated during a very long aging period in a series of casks of different woods without the addition of other aromatic substances. Its color is deep, shiny brown with a special density in the form of a runny syrupiness. Its characteristic perfume is complex and penetrating, showing a pleasant and harmonious acidity. Its sharp sweet flavor is full, sapid and velvety, in balance with its aroma."[89]

Only real balsamic is being discussed here unless otherwise
noted.

Traditionally, it is made by the lady of the house in Modena and
Reggio Emilia, which is the former territory of the former Domij
Estensi. This was once a duchy ruled by the Este Family. The
bulk of the vinegar is now produced in Modena and the area
south of Modena. The vineyards in these areas produce the best
grapes for making balsamic vinegar.

## ITALY

The precise method of making balsamic vinegar is difficult to
ascertain. "Those that know don't say and those that say don't
know." There are many "secret" recipes. This explanation of the
process, as well as the other information, is derived from
various literature on the subject.[90]

Some of the most important elements in producing a good
balsamic are the age of the batteria and the age of the vinegar. A
good balsamic must be at least 10 years old , although it is better
at 50, and almost perfect at 100. This means that the person who
starts the process will almost certainly be unaware of its final

quality. This also means that it is rather unlikely for it to be inexpensive.

Documents on balsamic vinegar date from 1747. However it is known that balsamics have existed long before that time. Barrels of balsamic vinegar belonging to families of Italian nobility contain vinegar whose production casks date as far back as 1630. A 3- ounce bottle of vinegar from those casks sold for $80 in California in 1985.

Balsamic vinegar comes only from grapes. The grapes may be from several types, including the Lambrusco, which is used extensively on the Emilian plains. But the Trebbiano di Spagna is generally preferred. This type of Trebbiano is quite different than the other Trebbianos of Italy. It matures fully and delivers a sweet juice.

This juice is filtered through cloth and placed in large copper pots and cooked slowly until it is condensed down to about two-thirds of the original content. After cooling, it is put into large barrels of Slavonian oak or chestnut for more than one year. This is where the alcoholic fermentation takes place.

The alcohol is then taken to the actaia. This is a special room, usually a well-ventilated attic, where the vinegars are exposed to summer heat and winter cold. These wide variations in temperatures are said to be essential to the development of a fine balsamic.

This new alcohol is then added to aged vinegar casks that have already been used for balsamic vinegar production. It is first added to a large barrel that already contains balsamic vinegar. A mother develops on the top of the vinegar. This mother is removed and washed every five to six years to remove any unwanted accumulations. It is unclear how important it is to wash and replace the mother that was removed. After the alcohol has been acidified, it is then transferred to a different barrel.

The succession of progressively smaller barrels made from various woods is called a batteria. The key to developing a fine balsamic vinegar is found in the batteria. Each barrel is made of special woods that contribute their subtle flavors to the product (see Woods for Aging vinegar appendix). Some of the older barrels were carved from a single piece of wood.

There may be from six to 12 or more different barrels through which the vinegar will pass during its gradual development. Each year, a small amount, often less than a liter, is taken out of the smallest cask. This cask is then replenished with younger vinegar from the next largest cask. Each cask is then replenished with younger vinegar from the progressively larger casks.

Not all of the producers agree on which woods or in which order the woods are to be used. Some people use only two types of wood, some use three or four types, and some people use as many as seven different types. The batteria of Francesco Ferretti of Fontana di Rubiera consist of one chestnut, two mulberry, and three oak casks. The batteria of Longhi of Castelfranco of Castelfranco-Emelia is made of two chestnut and two oak casks. The batteria of the Serafini acetaia in Modena is made up of five casks, all of Slovanian oak.

A typical batteria will be made up of chestnut and oak in the early stages and pass through barrels of diminishing sizes of chestnut, oak, cherry, locust, ash, mulberry and juniper. Oak and chestnut is used to impart tannins that color to the vinegar, cherry is used to add a delicate aroma and mulberry improves the aroma and density of the product. The aromatic woods are used at the beginning and the hard woods at the end of the process. Thin barrel staves are use to accelerate the acetification process and the thick ones to slow the process down. The ideal stave is about an inch thick.[91] The barrels will range from 50 down to 5 liters. All have an opening at the top to allow the vinegar bacteria to breathe. Sometimes, a piece of cheesecloth is placed over the top, but often only a wooden slab with a flat stone is used to keep out falling debris. During this process, extensive evaporation occurs, which leaves a vinegar with a consistency of syrup.

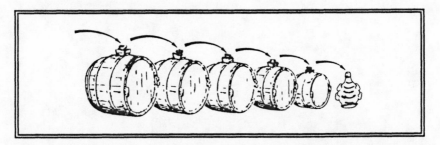

At the end of the process the vinegar is put into a round, narrow-necked crockery jug known as a tragn. This jug is distinguished by two sets of handles on both sides. Traditionally, it is further aged in these containers.

The fine flavor and high price limits this vinegar's use to only the most special occasions and recipes.(see uses section) There are many industrial versions around that can simulate but not duplicate the true balsamic. These imitation balsamics are useful in recipes where the subtleties of the true balsamics would be lost in the preparation process.

# SECTION THREE

# ENJOYING VINEGAR

# HERE COMES THE VINEGAR MAN
## SONG BY L.J. DIGGS

HERE COMES THE
VINEGAR MAN
TO HELP ALL HIS
VINEGAR FANS
HERE COMES THE
VINEGAR MAN
TO MAKE THIS A
VINEGAR LAND

IT'S THE MAN OF THE
HOUR
WITH HIS GREAT SOUR
POWER
IN HIS VINEGAR
DRESSINGS
HE BRINGS US GREAT
BLESSINGS

SO LETS HEAR IT NOW...

HERE COMES THE
VINEGAR MAN
TO HELP ALL HIS
VINEGAR FANS
HERE COMES THE
VINEGAR MAN
TO MAKE THIS A
VINEGAR LAND

GOT TO FIND OUT WHAT IT
TAKES
TO GET A PIECE OF THAT
VINEGAR CAKE

MAKE BAKE, BEG, BORROW OR
BUY
I GOT TO HAVE A PIECE OF THAT
VINEGAR PIE

CLEAN THE WINDOWS, WASH
THE CLOTHES
YOU CAN EVEN SCRUB THE
FLOORS

WITH VINEGAR!

FIRST HE PICKS THE FRUIT
WHEN IT'S GOOD TO EAT
THEN HE MAKES THE JUICE
MAKES IT OH SO SWEET

USE IT TO MAKE THE WINE
MAKE IT OH SO FINE
THEN HE REFINES THE WINE
WITH LOVE AND TIME

TO MAKE VINEGAR

SUPER SUPERLATIVE
FOOD PRESERVATIVE

ANTIBIOTIC
IF YOU SHOULD GET SICK

BALSAMIC
YOU CAN DIG IT

APPLE CIDER
MAKES YOUR LIFE SO MUCH
BRIGHTER

YOU USE IT FOR SALADS
YOU USE IT FOR DRINKS
TO FIX UP THE DINNER
AS QUICK AS A WINK

BUT YOU'VE GOT TO KNOW
HE'S GOT TO GO
BACK TO VINEGAR LAND

THERE HE GOES
BACK TO VINEGAR LAND

# CHAPTER 10

## FOOD USES

The vast majority of all vinegar produced is used for food, either in commercial production or home preparation. This fact is illustrated by the disposition of vinegar in the United States for 1985.

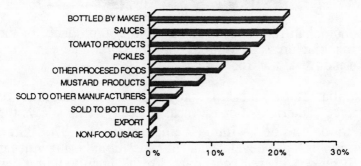

1985 DISPOSITION OF VINEGAR

## FIVE YEAR VINEGAR PRODUCTION PATTERN

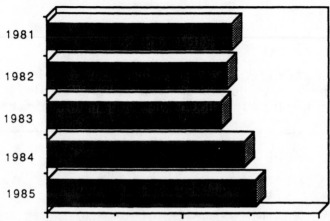

1981

1982

1983

1984

1985

Of the more than 166 million gallons of vinegar produced by the major manufacturers, only 136,557 gallons or .08 percent were sold for industrial non-food uses.

In Australia, diluted vinegar is sprayed on meats to kill many of the surface bacteria that cause meat to decay. This allows the meats to be shipped without being frozen[92]. The Ikilun corporation in Japan developed a "miracle" liquid using vinegar that will make withered vegetables "fresh" again within a few hours and keep them that way up to 10 times longer than normal.[93] Even the baking industry uses vinegar to as a mold inhibitor.[94] Japanese research has documented that microorganisms that cause colitis,dysentery and food poisoning are quickly killed by vinegar.[95]

Vinegar's taste enhancing characteristics make it ideally suited for food. It has the unique capability of carrying the flavors of other ingredients, such as herbs, spices and woods. It can also change the texture of foods, so it can be used to make cheese and other foods. Tofu, a soy milk cheese whose protein content compares favorably with meat, can also be made using vinegar.

Commercial manufacturers are using vinegar in almost everything that has a

tomato in it. It is used in almost every kind of sauce and spread. They are using it to flavor everything from sausage[96] to potato chips.[97]

It is estimated that up to 40 percent of the world's population will suffer from malnutrition. Even the rich and industrialized countries will be increasingly affected. Food preservation and food storage techniques will be critical in this struggle to relieve the world's unresolved and growing food crisis, and vinegar's use as a food preservative and sterilizing agent put it in a position to play a major role in this regard.[98]

Historically, one of the key factors that contributing to a culture's advancement was the acquisition of surplus food supplies. Since so many edible plants are seasonal and so many animals migratory, the preservation of food supplies were important. These surplus food supplies gave the cultures the leisure time and discretionary income needed to develop.

Many of the world's poorer nations use very little vinegar and manufacture even less. Vinegar can be very easily produced at, the commercial, village, and home level. It can be made from products that would otherwise be discarded in these countries. Its nutritional value alone makes it worth the effort.

The same preserving, sterilizing and flavor-enhancing properties that make it commercially valuable, make vinegar indispensable in kitchens around the globe.

Despite the fact that it is found in homes around the world, its full power is unknown and unused in most of those homes. Many spiced vinegars can be made that can serve as spices for vinegar cookery. This kind of cookery is well-suited for those on low-salt diets. Having four or more bottles of spiced vinegars readily available makes it possible to personalize each dish with a dash of vinegar. These are just a few of the ways in which vinegar can be used to improve or change the foods we eat.

## TASTE ENHANCEMENT

Because each type of vinegar carries with it a particular characteristic and personality, each lends itself to a particular use.

### CIDER VINEGAR

Cider vinegar is rather cloudy when made at home but is crystal clear when produced by companies that filter it. It finds a wide range of uses in the kitchen. It is often used as a substitute in dishes calling for Chinese or Japanese rice vinegar. However, since the Asian vinegars tend to be milder, it must be diluted slightly. It makes an excellent salad dressing. It should be used in any American recipe calling for vinegar unless otherwise specified.

Apple (Cider) Vinegar

Naturally cured Apple (Cider) Vinegar is a folk medicine from long ago and is still treasured
2 tablespoons in a glass of water (or Apple Juice) with a teaspoon of honey taken every morning was sworn by the early settlers as to relieve the pain from arthritis  dissolve calcium deposits  help in losing weight  aid in cleansing the blood  inhibits mastitis  fix an upset stomach or a headache  and many more
We cannot make such claims  but then we don t have to  the proof is in the trying
Just ask the good folks at your local  Diet Centre  and meet the results they are getting  and may the Lord bless you.

It is also the vinegar of choice in western medicinal preparations unless otherwise specified.

## WINE VINEGARS
Each wine vinegar will bring with it the particular characteristics of the fruit from which it was made. The most common divisions of wine vinegars are red, white, rosè and sherry. Red wine vinegar should be used in sauce hachee and sauce ala diable. Any of the wine vinegars can be used in bearnaise sauce.

Wine vinegars should be used in any European recipes calling for vinegar unless otherwise specified. They are excellent for flavoring with herbs, spices and fruits.

White wine vinegar is very good for making mayonnaise, lyonnaise, poivrade, hollandaise and ravigote sauce.

## MALT VINEGAR
This vinegar is popular for pickling, especially walnut pickles. It

is reported to be the vinegar used in the famous Worcestershire sauce. Sauce ala diable is made with malt vinegar in England. But it is most famous as the companion to fish and chips. Any English recipe calling for vinegar typically expects malt vinegar unless otherwise noted.

## DISTILLED VINEGAR
Because of the distillation process, distilled vinegars have no color and they very consistently contain 5 percent acetic acid. These particular characteristics lend themselves very well to pickling. The absence of color means that the item being pickled, particularly onions, will not change color. And the high percentage of acetic acid assures that the pickled item will be well preserved. Commercial food producers find this vinegar very useful in the preparation of various sauces where the finer qualities of other types of vinegars will be lost to the other ingredients and cost is of concern.

Because it is almost pure acetic acid, it is the vinegar of choice for non-food and medicinal uses. In addition to being less expensive, it does not contain materials that will leave films or residues.

It is often distilled from malt or apple cider vinegar but can be made from almost anything.

## SPIRIT VINEGAR
This kind of vinegar is made from snythetic alcohols, grains, wood sugars, molasses or sugar beets are also a distilled vinegar and therefore finds the same uses as distilled vinegars

## RICE VINEGAR
Rice vinegars come in a red, white, brown or black variety. They are excellent for flavoring with herbs spices and fruits. Unless otherwise indicated, they should be used in any Chinese or Japanese recipe calling for vinegar. They are generally lower in acetic acid strength than the other vinegars. they are great for dips and sauces, but caution is advised if these vinegars are to

be used for pickling, since the preservative action will be low. Some imported Chinese brands are as low as 2 percent!

Because it does not significantly alter the appearance of the food, white rice vinegar is the most widely used in Asian cooking. It is especially favored in soups and sweet-and-sour dishes.

The gaenmai or brown rice vinegar is generally the most flavorful of the rice vinegars when made by a reputable company. The best varieties are competitive with balsamics for smoothness, bouquet and taste. Its virtues as a medicinal agent have been rumored for centuries.

The red and black varieties are more common in Chinese cooking, where they are used more as a spice than a preservative.

Notice that it is not called rice <u>wine</u> vinegar. Since wine is made only from fruits,and rice is a grain, it cannot technically be called a wine vinegar.

## COCONUT AND CANE VINEGAR
These vinegars are common in India,the Philippines and Indonesia and are often the vinegars expected in recipes originating from those areas.

## DATE VINEGARS
These vinegars are frequently used in Middle Eastern recipes.

## FLAVORED VINEGARS

Vinegars flavored with fruits, herbs and spices such as tarragon, basil, lemon or thyme serve very well in the many vinaigrettes that can be made by a combination of these vinegars and oil. They also serve well in the creation of various sauces.

## VINAIGRETTES

The variety of vinaigrettes and other sauces that can be created from various vinegars and combinations of vinegars and spice are limited only by the imagination. The basic recipe is very simple, three or four parts oil to one part vinegar. But the combinations of vinegars oils and spices are endless.

Since many cookbooks include a large number of these recipes, their efforts will not be duplicated here. Cookbooks like the "Joy of Cooking" cover the subject of vinaigrettes quite well (see appendix for more complete list). Magazines and newspapers also frequently include unique recipes for vinegar-based sauces and dressings.

A few basic vinaigrettes will serve to give you the general idea of the variety and scope that this sauce covers.

### Vinaigrette à la crème
Add plain or whipped cream (to your taste) to a mixture of three parts seasoned oil and one part vinegar.

### Vinaigrette à la crème moutardee
Add mustard (to your taste)to the vinaigrette à la crème.

### Pork Vinaigrette
Add finely chopped bacon to the basic vinaigrette.

### Fish Vinaigrette
Save the juice from fish cooked in vinegar and mix it in equal parts with oil. This is great on Greek-type salads

Though the vinaigrette is most common as a salad dressing it can also be used as a marinade on fish, lamb or beef. Add garlic, onions, oregano and hot peppers, and suddenly it turns into a soup stock. A little alteration, and it's a salsa. [99]

## USE IN RECIPES

There are also a number of unusual recipes in which vinegar plays an important role. These recipes are not easy to find, so they are included here.

**Apple chutney**
Chutney adds a very nice touch to a meal of stew or curry, and it is relatively easy to make. There are many kinds of chutneys, some hot, some sweet, some sour and some with a combination of tastes. This one goes well with almost everything.


Assemble

> 2 pounds of peeled and cored apples
> 1 pound of raisins
> 1 pound of onions
> 1 pound of raw sugar
> 2 teaspoons of salt
> 1 teaspoon of cayenne
> 1 ounce of dry mustard
> 40 fluid ounces of vinegar

Coarsely chop all of these and mix them together. Put them into a large pot and boiled them for about one hour until they are tender. Pour them into preheated jars and seal.[100] Take all of the usual pickling precautions to assure safety and success (See pickling).

## Bread
To make a yeast raised bread that has a wonderfully unique taste and texture try this recipe.

Combine
>     2 cups of water
>     3 tablespoons of vinegar (4-5 percent in acid  strength)
>     2 teaspoons of salt

Warm this mixture to about 90 degrees F.

Now add
>     2 teaspoons of dry yeast
and wait until it foams. Then add this mixture to
>     5 1/2 cups of white flour

and knead until it is well-formed. Allow it to rise for about 15 minutes or until it has about doubled its volume. Knead again for about five minutes. Separate into two loaves and place in a cold oven. After about 10 minutes, turn the oven on to 350 degrees F and bake until brown.

Finishing touch on bread
To put a finishing touch on any home-made bread, take it out of the oven just before it is done, brush the top with your vinegar and then return it to the oven for the last few minutes.[101]

## Browning of fruits and potatoes
Place a little distilled vinegar in a bowl of water. As you cut the potatoes or fruit, place them into the water to keep them from turning brown.

## Cheese
Cheese can be kept moist and fresh by wrapping it in a cloth that has been dampened with vinegar and sealed in an air-tight wrap or container.[102]

(See  "vinegar cheese")

## Chicken adobo

This is a traditional dish from the Philippines. The principal flavor is derived from vinegar. It is a kind of vinegar stew and is typically served with rice. Cane and coconut vinegars are the common vinegars in the Philippines, but they are not necessarily the best . This dish is improved by using better vinegars, but it is delicious what ever vinegar is used. Other meats may also be substituted, but the cooking times will vary depending on which meat is used.

You will need;

1 chicken cut up into small pieces [with or without the head]

1 cup of vinegar
1 cup of water
2 tablespoons of soy sauce (Filipinos call this toyo)
1 bay leaf
5 cloves of crushed garlic
2 tablespoons of salt
5 peppercorns
2 mild red peppers.

Put everything into a pot and cook slowly until the chicken starts to come off of the bones and a gravy forms. If it is too sour for you, add a little more water. American chickens are fatter than their Filipino cousins, so you may want to remove some of the oil for health reasons.

## Chocolate cake (Made too easy)

This is about the easiest way possible to have chocolate cake without buying it ready-made. And look ma, no eggs.

Assemble;

3 cups of flour
2 cups of sugar

> 1/3 cup of cocoa
> 1 teaspoon of baking soda
> 1/2 teaspoon of salt
> 2 teaspoon of vinegar
> 2 teaspoons of vanilla
> 2/3 cup of oil
> 2 cups of water.

Mix all of the dry ingredients together in a large bowl, add the water and mix well. Now add the vinegar, vanilla and oil. Blend this mixture thoroughly and pour it into a 9-by-11-inch cake pan. Bake it for 30 minutes at 350 degrees F. Let it cool and eat.

### Fish
Before scaling fish, rub the fish down with distilled vinegar to make it easier to handle while reducing the fishy odor on the hands.[103]

### Fish sauce
To make a unique sauce for smoked fish, combine;

> 2 teaspoons of white vinegar
> 1/2 cup of sweet and heavy cream

Whip until stiff. [104]

### Flavor Booster
You can add a little zip to a can of soup, gravy or sauce by adding a teaspoon of your favorite vinegar. The taste of ordinarily bland foods can be enhanced with flavored or gourmet vinegars.[105]

### Fruit splash
Lightly splash balsamic or brown rice vinegar on fresh canteloup, sweet apples, pears or canned fruit to give a special zest to the flavor.[106]

Low calorie salad dressing
To make a low calorie salad dressing, Mix;

     1 cup of cottage cheese
     1/4 cup of skim milk
     1 teaspoon of your favorite vinegar.

Blend it for about a minute, then stir with a spoon and mix again. [107]

## Meat tenderizer
1. A marinade made of 1/2 cup of your favorite vinegar and a cup of liquid bouillon makes an effective meat tenderizer.

2. When you boil beef, do not forget to add about a teaspoon of your favorite vinegar to the water to soften the fibers and make the meat more tender.[108]

## Meringue
To make the meringue fluffier, add 1/4 teaspoon of distilled vinegar to each three to four egg whites.[109]

## Mustard
Mustard constitutes one of the major commercial uses of vinegar. Vinegar greatly enhances the taste of mustard while acting as a preservative at the same time. Many spices can be added to the mixture to arrive at an endless list of possibilities. These mustards, in turn, may be used as a quick way to flavor soups, salads, spreads and sauces.

To make mustard combine;

     2 ounces of dry mustard
     1 ounce of corn flour
     1/4 teaspoon of powdered ginger
     1/4 teaspoon of nutmeg
     1/4 teaspoon of ground cloves
     1/4 teaspoon of garlic powder
     1 teaspoon of salt
     1 tablespoon of honey
     1 cup of vinegar (Adjust amount depending on the

dryness of the other ingredients and desired taste.)

Mix everything into a thick paste and heat in a sauce pan. Simmer for about 1/2 hour. Allow to cool. Then store it for about 2 days before using.

Some makers claim that mustard should be made just before using. Others claim that its best virtues are developed after long aging. And, of course, there are 1,000 opinions everywhere in between. Dry mustard and vinegar are generally inexpensive enough to experiment with, so you can develop opinion 1001. Have fun.

## Odorless cabbage
The odor of boiling cabbage may be reduced if vinegar is added to the cooking water.[110]

## Overnight cucumber pickles
Assemble;

> 5 firm medium size cucumbers, about 3 pounds
> 1 3/4 teaspoons of salt
> 2 1/2 cups of cider or other vinegar
> 2 cups of sugar
> 2 teaspoons of mustard seed
> 1 teaspoon of celery seed
> 1 teaspoon of ground ginger
> 1 teaspoon of tumeric.

Slice the cucumbers into 1/2-inch slices. Place the sliced cucumbers into a large bowl, sprinkle with salt and mix well. Let it stand one hour. In a large sauce pot combine vinegar, sugar, mustard seed, celery seed, ginger and tumeric and bring them to a boil. Then drain the cucumbers well and add to the heated mixture. Let them simmer for about 10 minutes until tender. Pour into and container with a tight-fitting lid and refrigerate overnight.

## Poached eggs
Add a teaspoon of your favorite vinegar to the water in which you are poaching eggs to produce better-formed whites.[111]

## Quick buttermilk
If you find that you are out of buttermilk, you can make "instant buttermilk" by adding a teaspoon of white vinegar to each cup of sweet milk. Let it stand for about five minutes to thicken.[112]

## Quick pickles
Aside from being quick and easy to fix, these pickles have a unique "fresh" taste that gives them a special appeal with hot and spicy dishes like curry.

Slice the desired fruit or vegetable in the quantity needed. Pour flavored vinegar over the slices until they are well covered. Chill for an hour or more and serve. A small amount of sugar can add a nice touch to these pickles.

## Rice
A teaspoon of vinegar added to the water for boiling rice will make it white and fluffy.[113]

## Salad dressing (fruit)
Strawberry, raspberry or blueberry vinegar added to yogurt or sour cream makes a unique fruit salad dressing.[114]

## Sandwich spread
Sandwich spreads can be made by adding you favorite vinegar to mayonnaise to give it a special flavor. This trick can easily change an ordinary sandwich into a gourmet feast

## Secret sauce (Vinegar tasting dip)
Now you can make your own secret sauce. The secret is what kind of vinegar you use. This can be used as salad dressing, sandwich spread, boiled vegetable topping, you name it. And it can be as wild or as tame as you like. The only limitations are your imagination and the kinds of vinegar you have on hand.

This is also an ideal dip for vinegar tasting parties. Ten to 20 different dips and a few baskets of unsalted crackers or bread sticks and you are on your way to a unique event.

Secret Sauce can be made by adding;

> 1 teaspoon of your favorite vinegar
> to
> 4 tablespoons of mayonnaise

The exact proportions may be varied depending on the type of vinegar, the type of mayonnaise, and the desired taste.

Alternatively a **mayonnaise** can be made using the mayonnaise of choice. Mayonnaise can be made by putting;

> 1 egg
> 1 teaspoon of ground mustard
> 1 teaspoon of salt,
> 1 teaspoon of sugar
> 1/4 cup of salad oil
> 1 dash of cayenne

into a blender. Blend until it is completely mixed. While the blender is still running, remove the top and slowly drip in;

> 1/2 cup of salad oil.

Then slowly add

> 3 tablespoons of your favorite vinegar

and blend until it is well-blended. Slowly drip another

> 1/2 cup of salad oil

into the blender until it looks like mayonnaise. The mayonnaise may stick to the side of the blender. If so, stop the blender, stir down the mayonnaise and continue.

**Shrimp**
The "canned" taste of canned shrimp can be eliminated by
soaking the shrimp in a little sherry and 2 tablespoons of vinegar
for about 15 minutes.[115]

**Sweet and sour sauce**
This sauce finds itself on many different dishes. A white or
distilled vinegar makes the most straight forward version, but
don't be afraid to try other vinegars to add a different beat to an
old song.

Assemble;

>        2 tablespoons of soy sauce
>        3 tablespoons of vinegar
>        4 tablespoons of sugar
>        2 tablespoons of flour or corn starch
>        1 cup of water
>        1/8 teaspoon of salt.

Combine the flour and 1/4 cup of water in a sauce pan and mix
thoroughly. Then add all the other ingredients and mix them
well.

Now bring everything to a boil and simmer until it is thick
enough for your taste.

**Tea bag flavoring of vinegar**
A flavored vinegar can be made quickly and simply with tea
bags. Many prepared tea bags will impart particularly interesting
tastes to vinegars which can be used in a variety of ways,
including salads, soups and marinades. Do not expect the
sophistication of vinegars made in this way to compete with
those made by more labor intensive methods, but the taste will
be interesting. Experimentation pays dividends!

A tea bag can be purchased or it may be prepared using a small
piece of muslin or cheese cloth. The desired ingredients are

simply sewn or tied into the bag.

To flavor the vinegar, bring a 1/2 cup of vinegar to a boil and then remove the heat. Place the bags immediately into the hot vinegar and allow it to steep for about 15 minutes.[116]

## Tofu
Tofu can be made by using vinegar for the solidifier. The taste will not be as sour as might be expected. And the taste of the vinegar is often lost completely in the process. So do not use an expensive vinegar for this. (The making of tofu is beyond the scope of this book. "The Book of Tofu" by William Shurtliff is an excellent guide to making, using and appreciating tofu).

## Vegetables
Slightly wilted vegetables may be freshened by soaking them in cold water and vinegar.[117]

## Vinegar cake
Those who must avoid eggs will find vinegar cake of interest. In this cake, vinegar is used in place of the eggs to replace the effects of eggs on the texture of the cake. It also adds a pleasant taste to the cake.

Assemble;

> 3/4 cups of melted butter
> 3 cups of flour
> 1 cup of brown sugar
> 1 teaspoon of allspice
> 2 tablespoons of vinegar
> 1 tablespoon on baking soda
> 1 teaspoon of vanilla
> 1 cup of milk
> [optional chopped nuts and raisins]

Pour the melted butter and vanilla into the flour and mix until it forms tiny beads. Then add the sugar and allspice to the flour mixture. In a separate bowl, mix the baking soda and the milk.

Then add the vinegar and stir. Notice it is foaming. When it is covered with a beer-like head, add it to the other mixture. (This step is critical. If you are going to make an error it is better to do it too fast than too slow)

A 1/2 cup of chopped nuts and raisins will add a special touch to this treat.

The whole mixture is then poured into a greased and floured cake pan and baked at 350 degrees F. for 1 1/2 hours.

## Vinegar candy

Assemble

>2 tablespoons of butter
>2 cups of sugar
>1/2 cup of vinegar

Apple cider, brown rice or industrial (.i.e. cheap) balsamic are the choice vinegars for this recipe, but do not limit yourself. Even a distilled vinegar will make an interesting candy.

Melt the butter in a sauce pan. Now add the sugar and vinegar. Stir until the sugar dissolves. Wash down the sides of the pan with a pastry brush dipped in cold water. Boil the mixture until it becomes gooey, then pull or cut it into small pieces. Arrange the pieces on an oiled plate to cool.

## Togo toffee
They have probably never heard of this in Togo, but French toast was not invented in France, either. Anyway it sounds better than vinegar candy No. 2

Assemble;

>2 tablespoons of butter
>a pinch of salt
>a pinch of allspice

1/2 teaspoon of vanilla
2 cups of sugar
1/2 cup of vinegar

Apple cider, brown rice or balsamic are the preferred vinegars for this recipe, but again,do not limit yourself.

Melt the butter in a sauce pan. Now add the sugar, salt, allspice, and vanilla and vinegar. Stir until the sugar dissolves and begins to become brittle. Then remove and place it into a cold bowl of water. A ball will form. This ball can be pulled, stretched and cut into small pieces when it is cooled.

### Vinegar "cheese"
Technically speaking cheese made in the United States of America must be a result of action by microorganisms. A biological process. Since this product results from the action of a chemical agent (vinegar), it cannot, technically speaking ", be called cheese. But the difference between the two products is often hard to distinguish with the tongue. And unlike cheese, which takes days to years to complete, vinegar "cheese" can be made in a few minutes to a few hours, depending on how elaborate you want to get.

Warm a gallon of milk to about 95 degrees. Then add about 1 cup of vinegar, sprinkling about a tablespoon at a time. at two to five minute intervals. When you add the vinegar, stir very gently once. Then watch for curdles to form. When they stop forming, add a little more vinegar.

After some time you will notice that the curds and whey will have separated. When this has happened, strain off the whey through a cheese cloth and collander assembly. The white product will be your "cheese". Salt to taste, cool and enjoy.

## Vinegar cookies

Assemble;

> 2 cups of white flour
> 1/2 teaspoon of salt
> 1/2 teaspoon of baking soda
> 1/2 cup of sugar
> 1/2 cup of melted margarine
> 2 tablespoons of water.
> 1/4 cup of vinegar

Apple, balsamic or distilled vinegars are preferred, but others can be used

Mix all of the dry ingredients. Mix the vinegar and water together, then add the vinegar and water to the dry ingredients. Now add the melted butter. Stir and allow to stand for about 10 minutes. Form the cookies with a teaspoon and place on a greased and floured cookie sheet. Bake at 350 degrees F. until brown. Walnuts and/or almonds and raisins add a little something extra to these delicious cookies.

By the way, if anyone should ask, these are "African spice cookies" until after they are tasted.

## Vinegar drink (cold)

> 1 tablespoon of honey
> 1 ounce of apple cider vinegar
> 14 ounces of cold water.

OR

Stir a tablespoon of strawberry or orange vinegar into an 8-ounce glass of club soda and ice.

## Vinegar drink (hot)

     1 tablespoon of honey
     1 tablespoon of Balsamic vinegar
     cup of hot water

Mix the honey and vinegar in a cup or small tea pot. Pour in the hot water and serve. The recipe may be multiplied as long as the proportions are kept within reasonable limits. Reasonable limits are determined by your taste, so you have a lot of room to experiment.

The vinegar / honey mixture may be made up ahead of time by mixing one part honey with one part balsamic vinegar. warm slightly in a sauce pan. Pour into a bottle and cap tightly. When you want to use it, mix 2 tablespoons with each cup of hot water.

(Note: There is little reason to use the best balsamics for either of these drinks except on very special occasions. Other vinegars may also be used.)

**Vinegar pie**
There are a number of recipes for vinegar pie, but it is unusual to find them in cookbooks. If you make this pie for guests, you might want to give it another name. Vinegar pie, despite its delicious taste, does not sound very appetizing. "African Spice Pie" sounds a little more mysterious and appetizing. You may or may not want to let them in on your secret ingredient until <u>after</u> they have eaten it

Assemble;

     9-inch pie shell (See vinegar pie crust).
     4 eggs
     1 1/2 cup of sugar
     1/4 melted butter or margarine
     1 teaspoon of vanilla extract
     1 1/2 tablespoons of inexpensive balsamic vinegar

Any kind of vinegar can be used, but balsamic gives particularly good results.

Heat the oven to 350 degrees F. In a large mixing bowl put the
eggs, butter, sugar and vanilla and mix well. Pour these well-
mixed ingredients into the pie shell. Bake for about 50 minutes
until it is firm. Allow it to cool. Then add topping of nuts,
meringue (see meringue) or whipped cream. This pie may also
be served without a topping.

### Vinegar pie crust

This crust is good for any kind of pie where a nice flaky crust is
desired.

Assemble;

> 3 cups of flour
> 1 cup of shortening
> 1/2 teaspoon of salt
> 1 egg
> 5 tablespoons of cold water
> 1 tablespoon of white or apple cider vinegar.

In a large bowl, mix the flour, shortening and salt with a fork or
pastry cutter until small crumbs about the size of small peas are
formed.  Beat the egg with a fork and mix it with the cold water
and vinegar. Pour this liquid mixture into the large bowl and
mix well until a ball of dough is formed. Divide the dough into
three balls of equal size. Each of these balls should make a 9-
inch pie crust. Roll out the dough and bake at 425 degrees F.
until it is slightly brown.

The unneeded dough may be stored in the refrigerator or freezer.
It should be allowed to come to room temperature before any attempt is made to use it.

## White sauce

1/4 teaspoon of your favorite vinegar, added to a cup of white sauce will intensify the flavor.[118]

## PICKLING TIPS

Pickling constitutes one of the major uses of vinegar. However, a complete treatment of the subject is beyond the scope of this book. There are many books that cover the subject well. Check the appendix for suggestions of other books on pickling.

To obtain an easy-to-use guide to pickling, Write to;

The Vinegar Institute
P.O. Box 720215
Atlanta Georgia

or

Consumer relations
Heinze U.S.A.
P.O. Box 57
Pittsburgh PA 15230

## Materials for Pickling
Bruised and moldy vegetables and fruit frequently result in less-than-acceptable pickles and should therefore be avoided. Fruits for pickling should be slightly underripe. When possible, they should be pickled within 24 hours after harvesting. Whole cucumbers should have a quarter inch of stem left on the end. Wax-coated cucumbers will not work for pickling because the vinegar cannot penetrate the wax.[119]

## Salt
Pickling salt must be used in any pickling recipe calling for it. Table salt contains iodine and will darken the pickles. Anti-caking additives in table salt will cloud the pickling liquids and interfere with fermentation. Rock salts or other salts used to melt ice on the roads or sidewalks often contain industrial contaminants.[120]

## Acetic acid strength
Make sure that the acetic acid strength of the vinegar is at least 4.5 percent - 5 percent . The vinegar will draw water from the fruit or vegetable in the pickling process. This will lower the strength of the pickling solution. If the strength of this solution falls to a point where it loses its preservative qualities, the pickles may spoil, or worse, may become contaminated with dangerous microorganisms.[121]

## Accurate measurements
Be sure to measure the ingredients accurately. Too much of one ingredient and too little of another may result in pickles that are unsafe or taste poor.[122]

## Dark vinegars
Cider, red wine, balsamic and other dark vinegars are very good for pickling but may discolor lighter-colored pickles such as pears, onions or cauliflowers. In this case, a distilled or white vinegar may be preferred.

## Altering the recipe
Decreasing the amount of vinegar in a recipe to reduce the amount of sourness may result in pickles that have less preservative action than is necessary for safety. Another recipe should be used instead.[123] Diluting the pickles just before using also works.

## Spices
Fresh spices assure the best taste. Old or improperly stored herbs and spices often deteriorate and lose flavor.[124]

## Utensils
Copper, brass, iron, aluminum or galvanized utensils will often react with vinegar, changing the color or forming dangerous compounds, and therefore are to be avoided.

## Jars
Discard used jars that have chipped necks or mouths. They will not be able to form a tight seal. Make sure that the sealing compound on the new metal lids is smooth and even.[125]

# CHAPTER 11

## MEDICAL USES

Vinegar's use as a medicine goes back to ancient times[126]. Due to its antimicrobial properties, (it kills or retards the growth of microorganisms), it has been used as an antibiotic for the dressing of wounds as well as other uses. Throughout those years, vinegar has been suggested as a cure or ingredient in a cure for most human and many animal ailments. While many of those claims have withstood the test of time and scientific scrutiny, some have proved to be baseless, even ridiculous. One proponent of vinegar as a cure of yellow fever died of yellow fever[127].

It is not the intent of this chapter to suggest using vinegar in place of seeking competent medical advice. However, you will discover in this chapter that renowned physicians have recommended vinegar for a wide variety of ailments for many centuries.

In an article titled "Vinegar: Building Block for the Body," various scientists reported their findings on vinegars role in human metabolism. This article pointed out that as a result extensive scientific study, vinegar was shown to be an extremely valuable constituent in the body's biochemical operations. The article pointed out that vinegar is an essential building block in the construction of many complex substances in the body. This research was carried out in four different universities.[128]

One study used tagged atoms to trace the path of vinegar through the tissues and cells, allowing the scientist to discover how the body uses it. It was found that acetic acid, the principal constituent in vinegar, played an important role in the release of energy from fats and carbohydrates. Vinegar also participated in the development of fats, glucose, amino acids and hemoglobin (the red pigment in the blood that supplies the body with oxygen). These reports were delivered in a meeting of the American Chemical Society.[129]

Dr. Konrad F. Block of the department of biochemistry in the College of Physicians and Surgeons at Columbia University, said, "Acetic acid (vinegar) has only recently been recognized to be of primary importance in the bodys' metabolism. He added, "Normally, part of it is carried by the blood into the kidney and muscle and undergoes complete oxidation with the release of energy. Some is retained and utilized as a source of carbon atoms for the synthesis of a variety of tissue constituents."[130]

Dr. F. Lipman of the Biochemical Research Laboratory of Massachusetts General Hospital reported that "when foreign substances such as drugs are introduced into the body, acetic acid frequently reacts by trying to detoxify them. It unites the toxic substances with other molecules to produce a new compound. The combination of sulfanomides with acetate forms a compound that is biologically inactive and more easily excreted."[131]

In the Journal of the American Medical Association, Dr. Irving L. Ochs of Annapolis Maryland reported on the use of vinegar to treat external otitis, a severe form of ear infection. He said that "acetic acid acts specifically as a bacteriacidal agent against *B. pyocyaneus* . It is frequently used as a wet dressing to over come infections in contaminated surgical wounds, burns, and granulating osteomeylitic wounds due to this organism. A solution containing 1 to 2 percent acetic acid clears the malodorous green discharge in a few hours. There is no apparent damage to the tissue with this treatment.[132]"

He also cited an article by Dr. C. R. Owen[133] in which Dr. Owen demonstrated the bacteriacidal properties of acetic acid against gram-negative bacteria. Owen found that .1 cc of 10 percent acetic acid in a media of 15 cc of a beef heart broth will completely inhibit the growth of gram negative bacilli.

However, *Streptococci* and *Staphylococci* will continue to grow. He pointed out that this was the result of acetic acid and not just acid alone, since hydrochloric acid and sulphuric acid did not give the same results.

Dr. Ochs devised a technique which was essentially to clean the ear using hydrogen peroxide to loosen any debris and discharges. After the ear is cleaned, it is stuffed with cotton and saturated with household vinegar of 5 percent strength. The patient keeps this ear plug saturated with vinegar and an aluminum acetate solution. After 48 hours, the patient returns and the wick is removed. If there is still pain and swelling, the patient continues the treatment for another 48 hours. If the condition is chronic, it may require a week or more before the skin returns to normal.[134]

He presented the following case as representative of his findings.

A 40-year-old man had had a discharging ear for five years. He had been treated with dyes, silver nitrate, sulfanomide drugs, rotegen rays and physiotherapy without any success. Within hours of the use of the acetic acid tampon, the discharge stopped completely. The swelling of the canal was reduced enough to permit adequate cleaning. The wet dressing and cleaning regimen was continued until there was an absence of swelling. The patient was told to apply an ointment that kept his ear dry, smooth, open and relatively free of itching.

Och concluded that this technique using vinegar is an effective, available and inexpensive way to control external otitus.[135]This treatment is now standard for this disease when it is caused by *Pseudomonas, Candida, or Aspergillus.*[136]

The modern medical profession has found that 5 percent concentrations of acetic acid is lethal to many microorganisms. Lower concentrations have also been found to be quite effective in medical treatment. In 1 percent solutions, it is used prophylactically in surgical dressings, and a .25 percent solution is used in catheterization and irrigation of the bladder. Vaginal infections caused by *Candida* and *Trichomonas* are treated with douche solutions of 0.25 percent to 1 percent. These solutions are also used as a spermatocide. Concentrations of 5 percent have been found to be effective in treating extensive burns when there is a need to suppress the growth of *Pseudomonas aeruginosa*. These solutions are sometimes irritating to the vagina and concentrations of more than 5 percent are sometimes irritating to the skin.[137]

But the documentation of the effectiveness of vinegar as a medication goes back as far as Hippocrates, who is often called the father of modern medicine. [138] He used vinegar in the treatment of a number of illnesses. Oxymel, a medicine often prescribed, was a combination of honey and vinegar.[139] He instructed his students that they would find the drink called oxymel very useful for promoting expectoration and freedom of breathing. When strongly acid, the oxymel helps to make coughing productive.[140]

Hippocrates also prescribed oxymel for a chronically constipated patient who has a fever.[141] It was also recommended in the treatment for peripneumonia and pleuritic affections.

Oxyglyky is decoction of honeycombs and vinegar.[142] It was recommended in the treatment of an acute separation of the heel.

Vinegar itself was recommended in the treatment for inflammations and swellings, ulcers of various types and burns. In one remedy Hippocrates detailed a vinegar preparation for cleaning ulcerations.[143] Vinegar compresses were also recommended in the treatment of sores.

Variations of the oxymel formula has found favor among physicians right up through modern times. In the second century A.D., the great physician Galen also prescribed the combination of honey and vinegar for coughs. In 1703, B. Boyles, a fellow of the Royal Society of London recommended it as a gargle.

More recently Dr. D.C. Jarvis also recommended it his book "Folk Medicines" for a wide variety of ailments.

## USE IN ASIA

The medicinal use of vinegar is not limited to western medical practice. Vinegar is called the friend of Chinese herbs because it is often used to process the herbal preparations. It is added to enhance the desired effects and inhibit the the undesired effects. It is thought to possess yin qualities and is used to arrest bleeding, disperse blood coagulation and counteract toxic effects, as well as a variety of other herbal cures.[144]

Modern Chinese medicine also uses vinegar. The Hu Bei Yeecang People's Hospital treated 51 cases of jaundice hepatitis with 10 ml. of rice vinegar and two vitamin B-1 tablets. All of the patients recovered in four days and regained their appetites. [145]

The Research Institute of Epidemic Diseases at the Chinese academy of Medical Science conducted an experiment on the use of vinegar to treat respiratory infections. They cultured 200 colonies of microorganisms known to cause such diseases as pneumonia, influenza and catarrh. Most of those bacteria were killed within 30 minutes in an atmosphere of vaporized vinegar. This experiment may explain why the workers in the vinegar division were the only ones spared when an epidemic of influenza struck a food plant in China. Another report from a Chinese food processing plant claims that an average of 8 percent of their workers suffer respiratory infections per year while only 1 percent of those who work in the vinegar section suffer such illnesses. And the report say's that the workers in the vinegar section suffer less when they are stricken.[146]

There are also reports that Japan[147] and India make medicinal use of vinegar. [148]

## COMMON CONDITIONS HISTORICALLY CURED
## BY VINEGAR

To make a complete list of all of the conditions that have been reported to have been cured by vinegar would be difficult if not impossible. However, a review of the more common conditions for which vinegar has been a time honored cure is found below. It must be emphasized that these are not recommendations. These are <u>reports</u> of recommendations. The best advice is to consider the source and consult competent medical practitioners. It is for this reason that the sources have been carefully documented in the footnotes.

**Abdominal pain**
To relieve lower abdominal pain, mix a little salt with a little vinegar and drink.[149]

**Alcoholism**
Dissolve 15 grams of sugar in a little hot water and mix with 30 ml of rice vinegar. [150]

**Antidote for poison**
When the patient has been injured by exposure to or ingestion of alkaline substances, the neutralizing effect of vinegar can be used as an antidote.[151] e.g. Drink or apply vinegar to counteract the damaging effects of lye poisoning.[152]

**Asthma**
Peel three whole heads of garlic and add to a sauce pan of 2 1/2 cups of water. Simmer this combination until half of the water is gone. Remove the garlic and add 1 1/4 cup of apple cider vinegar to 1/4 cup of sugar. Stir and boil this until it becomes a syrup. Put the cloves into a jar and pour the syrup over them. Take one or two cloves of the garlic with a teaspoon of the syrup every morning.[153]

**Birth control**
Douche with vinegar.[154]

**Bleeding**
1. Apply a paste of vinegar and wheat flour. 2. Apply a towel soaked in vinegar and salt.[155]

**Blood purifier**
Eat a salad of raw onions dressed with salt and vinegar.[156]

**Bronchitis**
Bathe the chest with a mixture of one part hops and two parts vinegar.[157]

**Burns**
1. Apply apple cider vinegar[158] [159]. 2. Apply a poultice of vinegar and bran boiled together.[160]

**Chapped hands**
A mixture of 1 tablespoon of glycerine,10 drops of floral oil and 5 tablespoons of vinegar is applied to the hands while damp after washing. This should be done two or three times daily.[161]

**Cold sores**
Take a copper penny that has been soaked in vinegar and touch the sore with it several times.[162]

**Colds**
1. Take a lump of butter, a little pepper, a half cup of syrup and a teaspoon of vinegar and mix all together. (presumably this is drank but no instructions as to its use was given). 2. Inhale boiling vinegar.

3. Rub vinegar over the painful parts to relieve the pain. [163] 4.The inhalation of vinegar fumes, produced by heating the vinegar, is done to clear the head in the case of a cold. Ancient Romans inhaled vinegar fumes after stepping out of a bath.[164]

Add 15 grams of peeled and crushed garlic to 15 ml of rice vinegar and serve to the patient with his noodles.

## Colds (baby)
Dip the baby's sock in vinegar and tie it around the baby's neck. (not too tight ) [165]

## Colic
Place a poultice of hops and vinegar on the stomach.[166]

## Corns
1. Apply poultice of bread crumbs and vinegar to the corn. 2. Pour vinegar on the hinge of a door right after you have seen a shooting star.[167] 3 Pour two teaspoons of vinegar into an egg cup and drop a piece of copper wire into it. Let it stand for two days and paint the corns with the vinegar-soaked wire once or twice per day. The corns will soften and can be lifted out painlessly.[168]

## Coughs

1. One quart of cider vinegar and 1 pound of brown sugar is mixed and boiled until it is reduced to one pint. When it is cool, add a little paregoric and use as cough syrup. 2. Heat butter, salt, sugar, pepper and vinegar together and take as cough syrup.[169] 3. Boil together in 3 pints of water a sprig of horehound, two lemons, one broken stick of liquorice, 3 table-spoons of linseed, 1 cup of honey, 1/2 pound of raisins and 2 tablespoons of vinegar (use as a cough syrup).[170]

## Croup

1.Heat butter, sugar and vinegar together. 2. Eat vinegar and butter. 3. Take a little sugar and butter and add it to 1/4 cup of vinegar and water. Heat and drink to take away the phlegm. 4. Heat two parts hops with one part vinegar, make a poultice and apply to the chest.[171] 5. Beat together 1 teaspoon of sulphur, 1 teaspoon of vinegar and the white of one egg. Wrap the patient in a blanket, elevate the head and give him the mixture.[172]

## Drug preparation

Vinegar often appears in old drug preparations simply because it was one of the only weak acid solvents available at that time. In the eighteenth century, "Quakers Black Drop" was made from wild crab apple vinegar and opium. Wood ashes and vinegar was used by the Greeks and Romans for various skin ailments. The medical practitioners of India have also used vinegar as a solvent for drugs.[173]

## Dysentery

Add fresh cut and peeled radishes to rice vinegar and sugar. Eat the radishes twice a day.[174]

### Ear ache
Hold the ear over a steaming mixture of vinegar and water.[175]

### Fainting
When a child loses conciousness when in convulsions with rapidly decreasing temperatures, vinegar is boiled at a high heat in a closed room so that the child inhales the vaporized vinegar. The same procedure is used to awaken women who faint after childbirth.

### Fever
1.Mix corn flour, black pepper, powdered garlic and vinegar. Compress this mixture on the calves of the legs and feet. 2. Bathe the patient in vinegar and salt. [176] 3. In the United States and Russia among other places, patients are bathed with diluted vinegar to lower a fever.[177]

### Freckle removal
Apply vinegar to the freckle.[178]

### Fungus infections
1. Apply vinegar 3 times per day to the affected area.[179] 2. For severe cases involving the hand, tie a plastic bag filled with vinegar around the hand and let it remain overnight.[180]

### Hair care
1. After washing the hair, rinse it with water containing several tablespoons of vinegar[181]. This vinegar may be scented by various herbs and spices. 2. Vinegar rubbed onto the scalp

relieves dandruff in two ways. It kills bacteria associated with dandruff and helps to eliminate traces of soap left after the hair is washed. It is recommended that it be applied nightly at first and then gradually discontinued as the condition improves. [182]

## Hand care
Apply poultice of flax seed meal and vinegar to the hand and tie the hand inside a plastic bag to relieve pain and swelling.[183] Moisture can be restored to hands which have been damaged by strong cleaning solutions, plaster, concrete or detergents by rubbing them in distilled vinegar.[184] Apply lemon juice and vinegar to eliminate brown spots on white skin.[185]

## Hay fever
The inhalation of one part freshly ground horse radish and one part vinegar (by volume) is advised for the alleviation of the symptoms of hay fever. It should be inhaled three or four times daily. [186]

## Headache
1.Put Jimson weed in a folded cloth, wet the cloth with vinegar and apply to the forehead. 2. Wet the top of the head with cider vinegar. 3. wet cloth with vinegar and tie ti around the head. 4. Wet cloth with hot vinegar and apply to the top of the head. [187]

## Heartburn
Mix soda and vinegar. (presumably this is drank)[188]

## Hepatitis
1. Add 500 grams of pork spareribs, 125 grams of brown sugar, 125 grams of white sugar to 4 cups of rice vinegar. Boil these together for no more than 30 minutes and strain our the liquid. For children, 5-10 years old, give 10 to 15 ml, for those 11-15, give 20 to 30 ml, and for those over 15 give 30 to 40 ml.

Each of these doses should be given 3 times per day after meals for one month. For chronic patients 2 to 3 treatment programs may be required.[189]

## Herbal bath
Combine 1 tablespoon of dried lemon balm, 1 tablespoon of dried mint and 1 tablespoon of dried thyme. Gently boil a mixture of 1 cup of apple cider vinegar and one cup of water. Remove the liquid from the heat and add the herbs. Allow it all to steep for 8 hours or more. Strain it well and place it in a tightly sealed container. Use 1 cup full in each bath.[190]

## Hiccoughs
Add a teaspoon of vinegar to hot water, stir in one teaspoon of soda and drink while it is still foaming.[191]

## Hiccups
Combine 20 ml of cold water and 20 ml of rice vinegar and drink it slowly.[192]

## High blood pressure
Eat celery cooked with vinegar as a spice.[193] Soak 10 peanuts in a cup of vinegar overnight. Drink the vinegar and eat the peanuts the next morning. Repeat this treatment for 10 to 15 days.[194]

## Increased alcohol tolerance

Two universities and the Nakano vinegar company in Japan have done research which indicate that the consumption of a little vinegar will enable the consumption of a lot of alcohol.[195]

## Indigestion

Baking soda and vinegar diluted in water.[196] Add vinegar to meats to stimulate the appetite and promote digestion. [197]

## Infertility

Drink honey and vinegar.[198]

## Inflammation

Place a piece of brown paper bag which has been soaked in vinegar on the affected area.[199]

## Influenza

Soak 250 grams of fresh radish in vinegar and eat as a salad.[200]

## Insect bites

Apply household vinegar directly to the bite to stop the itching and stinging. This works because some insect bites are painful because the insects poison consists of alkaline substances. Applying vinegar neutralizes the poison thus relieving the pain.[201 202]

## Kidney problems

Put rusty nails in vinegar drink.[203]

## Leg pain

Drink half cup of vinegar in hot water. [204]

## Lice
Grease the head with bacon grease, wash with soap and rinse with vinegar. Repeat weekly until lice (or hairs) are gone.[205]

## Menstrual period problems
Mix the white of an egg with 3 teaspoons of rice vinegar to continue menstruation after bearing a child.[206]

## Morning sickness
Add 30 grams of sugar to 60 ml of boiling water and stir until dissolved. Cook one broken egg in this mixture and, when it cool enough, drink it all.[207]

## Mouth infection
Chop and boil grass, plantain leaves and red beet tops, add them to vinegar and make a poultice by thickening with flour. Apply to the affected area.[208]

## Mouth wash
The addition of a bit of salt into diluted vinegar is recommended as a mouth wash.[209] Mix 1/2 teaspoon of vinegar in 1/2 glass of warm water.[210]

## Muscle relaxer
The addition of vinegar to bath water will help to relax the muscles. Scents of various herbs and spices can be added to the vinegar to make the bath even more enjoyable.[211]

## Nausea
The inhalation of vinegar fumes, produced by heating the vinegar, is said to relieve nausea.[212]

## Neuralgia
1. Add 1/4 ounce of mustard oil, 1 ounce of peppermint, the white of one egg to one pint of vinegar and shake well. Rub this mixture on the affected spot. 2. Make a paste of red pepper and vinegar, spread it on a cloth and apply to the affected area.[213]

## Night sweats
Bathe the body in a cupped handful of vinegar just before going to bed.[214]

## Pain (general)
Flax seed meal and vinegar poultice is applied to affected area.[215]

## Palate (fallen or swollen)
Put vinegar on a spoon and use the spoon to lift the palate.[216]

## Panacea
Vinegar and honey.[217]

## Pimples
Make a paste of wheat flour, honey and vinegar and apply to the pimples.[218]

## Plague
During the infamous plague which raged through Europe, four men were caught and sentenced to the gallows for robbing and murdering people in infected houses. They claimed that they had

escaped infection themselves by using this preparation.

"Take of rue, sage, mint, rosemary, wormwood and lavender, a handful of each, insure them together in a gallon of white wine vinegar, put the whole into a stone pot closely covered up, upon warm wood ashes for four days: After which draw off (or strain through fine flannel) the liquid, and put it into Bottles well corked; and into every quart bottle put a quarter of an ounce of camphor. With this preparation, wash your mouth, and rub your loins and your temples every day, sniff a little up your nostrils when you go out into the air, and carry about a bit of sponge dipped in the same, in order to smell upon all occasions especially when you are near any place or person that is infected"

This preparation was found in a book of recipes by an anonymous writer dated 1747. It has been variously referred to as "The Medicine" or "The Vinegar of the Four Thieves". [219]

### Pleurisy
Bran and vinegar poultice is applied to affected area.[220]

### Pneumonia
Onion and vinegar poultice is applied to the chest.

### Poison ivy
Mix 1 cup of apple cider vinegar and 1 cup of water. Apply often to the affected part and allow to dry on the skin.[221]

### Rheumatism
1.Mix honey and apple cider vinegar, and drink every morning.
2. Apply a plaster made of red clay and vinegar to the affected area.[222]

## Ring worm

1. Drink a tea made of equal parts of burdock roots and vinegar several times per day until the ringworm is gone. 2. Rub an old copper penny, which has been soaked in vinegar, over the affected area. 3. Apply a paste made of gunpowder and vinegar to the affected area and leave it until the ringworm is gone.[223] 4. Many people in the Ozarks insist that rubbing vinegar on ring worm hastens the recovery from that disease.[224] 5. Mix baking soda and and strong vinegar and apply to the ringworm.[225] 6. Apply apple cider vinegar directly to the ring worm 6 times per day between the time the patient arises until he goes to bed.[226]

## Roundworms

Mix 40 ml of rice vinegar and 40 ml of warm water. Drink ths dosage 3 times per day for three days.[227]

## Shaving lubricant

A shaving lubricant can be made with three parts distilled white vinegar, one part citrus fruit juice and a little vitamin E. This lubricant will reduce nicking, cutting and chafing of the skin due to shaving. It is also said to slow the regrowth of the beard [228].

## Shingles

Apply apple cider vinegar to the affected area four time per day and three times per night if you awake.[229]

## Skin toner

The addition of vinegar to the bath water will tone up the skin and leave it free from soap residues. Scents of various herbs and spices can be added to the vinegar to make the bath even more enjoyable.[230]

## Sore throat

1. Put 2 cups of raspberries in a bowl and pour 2 1/2 cups of white wine vinegar over them. Stir, cover and leave for 4 days. Then stir in 1 cup of sugar and bring the mixture to a gentle boil. continue stirring and simmering for 20 minutes. Allow to cool,

strain, and bottle. Use the liquid as needed to relieve sore throat.[231]2. Drink and/or gargle with honey and vinegar. 3. Gargle with plain vinegar, 4. Gargle with vinegar and salt, 5. Gargle with vinegar and black pepper, 6. Gargle with vinegar salt and black pepper. 7. Make a syrup by boiling sugar, ginger, salt butter water and vinegar. Swallow a spoonful slowly as needed. 8. Soak rag in vinegar and wrap around the neck. 9. Boil a hand full of green sage leaves, strain and mix the liquid well with a teaspoon of black pepper, teaspoon of salt, a small piece of alum and a table spoon of vinegar. Gargle with this tea every half hour. 10. Dip a slice of bacon in vinegar, wrap it in cloth and apply to the throat.

### Sores
Soak a limb of a tree in vinegar until the vinegar turns brown and apply the vinegar to the sores.[232]

### Sprains
1. Make a liniment by boiling wooly mullein salt and vinegar together. Apply to sprain. 2. Cook two parts smart weed with one part vinegar and pack the mixture around the affected area[233]. 3. Vinegar soaked brown paper, bound around the sprained area has been used to treat sprains. Another variation of this remedy is to heat and add salt to the vinegar before soaking the paper in it.[234] 4. Another remedy is to "take the strongest vinegar you can get and boil it in a convenient quantity of wheat bran till you have brought it to the consistency of a poultice. Apply this as early as possible to the part affected and renew it when it begins to dry."[235] [236] 5. Bruise a hand full of sage leaves and simmer them gently tow-thirds cup of vinegar for five minutes. Remove the mixture from the heat and soak it up in a cloth. Apply the cloth as warm as possible to the affected part.[237]

## Sun burn
Soak a thin towel in distilled vinegar. Squeeze it out just enough to keep it from dripping profusely. Open it up and place over the burn for relief.[238] Note that this will not prevent sun burns.

## Swelling
1. Apply poultice of flax seed meal and vinegar. 2. Apply poultice of brown paper and vinegar to. 3. Add vinegar to a powder of red clay brick and apply to affected area. [239]

## Thrash
Add alum, turpentine and vinegar to a tea made with the bark of a privet tree. Wash the mouth with this tea.[240]

## Tooth ache
Hold vinegar in the mouth next to the affected tooth.[241]

## Typhoid fever
Rub patient with hot vinegar.[242]

## Ulcers
Mix wheat bran, black pepper, vinegar and turkey dung , apply to ulcers.[243]

Go light on the turkey dung!

## Vaginal douche
A douche solution of 4 tablespoons of distilled vinegar in two quarts of warm water is used to clear up ordinary cases vaginal discharges and restore vaginal acidity.[244] 1 ounce of white vinegar in one quart of warm water.[245]

## Varicose veins
Apply apple cider vinegar using the cupped hands treatment to shrink the veins. Combine this treatment with the consumption of two teaspoons of vinegar per day. Improvement should be noticed in about one month.[246]

## Warts
1. Soak old copper penny in vinegar and rub over the wart. Then throw the penny away. 2. Place a ball of flint marble in a bottle filled with vinegar and bury the contents. 3. If you hold a toad wash your hands with vinegar right away to avoid the warts.[247] count the number of warts you have, and take as many ants, and bind them up in a thin cloth with a snail, and bring all to ashes, and mingle them with vinegar. Take off the head of a small ant, bruise the body between you fingers, and rub with it any imposthumated tumor, and it will immediately sink down. [248]

## Wasp stings
Apply soda and vinegar to the affected area.[249]

## Weight loss
1. Take a teaspoon of vinegar each morning. 2. Drink a half glass of vinegar every day[250].

## Whooping cough
1. Place an egg in a pint of vinegar and leave until the shell is dissolved. Take a spoonful of this from time to time. 2. Take salt red pepper and vinegar.[251]

For more information on the health benefits of vinegar, please consult the writings listed in the footnotes and bibliography.

## VINEGAR AND ANIMALS

The use of vinegar for animals other than humans has not received much attention. But since it is such a common item around farms, it was inevitable that it be experimented with by farmers seeking to improve the condition of their animals. The results of that experimentation have been passed by word of mouth rather than scientific journals or books, so occasionally something gets lost, or gained, in the transmission. As with the human cures, there are those who swear the cures work and those who swear that they do not. They are included here because;

---

**"Resistant rumors should be researched because even the biggest lie contains an element of truth"**[252]

---

### Acetonaemia
To prevent this condition, 2 fluid ounces of vinegar are given to cows twice per day beginning three to six weeks before calving and continuing until four to six weeks after birth. To cure the disease,1/2 to 3/4 pints of vinegar is given depending on the size of the animal.[253]

### Farrowing fever
To prevent the fever two to three ounces per day are given to the sow starting from three weeks before she gives birth to two weeks after the birth. To cure the fever, she should be given two ounces per day for at least ten days.[254]

### Fertility improvement
Bulls are said to maintain semen of high fertility if given 4 fluid ounces of vinegar per day. 4 fluid ounces per day are recommended by some people for cows. Others suggest 1 pint just before serving.[255]

## Goats
Generally the cures for cattle can be used for goats if the dosages are cut in half.[256]

## Horses and ponies
The addition of three to six ounces of vinegar per day, depending on the size of the animal, is recommended to stimulate the appetite, improve the coat and stop dung eating.[257]

## Sprains
Put some brown paper over the affected area and pour hot vinegar over it.[258]

## Mastitis
Give the affected cow a daily ration of up to 8 fluid ounces per day for three days and then continue the dosage at half that amount, the condition should clear up with in seven days.[259]

## Milk fever
4 ounces of cider vinegar per day are given to the affected cow starting from six weeks before and continuing until three weeks after calving.[260]

## Pests off the pets
To help keep your pet free of fleas and ticks, add a teaspoon of vinegar for each quart bowl of drinking water. This ration is for a forty pound animal.[261]

## Poultry
It is reported that chickens and turkeys grow faster and have better egg shell development when a teaspoon of vinegar is mixed with a quart of their drinking water.[262]

# CHAPTER 12

## GENERAL USES

Throughout history vinegar has been used for science and industry. Alchemists have prized it for its many important properties[263], and modern industry uses it in many processes, including the manufacture of plastics.

It should come as no surprise, then, that it can be used in many everyday chores around the house. Its key constituent, acetic acid, makes it useful in cleaning, deodorizing and many other tasks. These are a few of the ways in which it can help you to live a more pleasant life.

## HOUSEHOLD USES

### Aluminum discoloration
The minerals found in foods and water will often leave a dark stain on aluminum utensils. This stain can be removed by boiling a solution of 1 tablespoon of distilled vinegar per cup of water in the utensil. Utensils may also be boiled in the solution. [264]

### Ant deterrent
Ant invasions can sometimes be deterred by washing counter tops, cabinets and floors with distilled vinegar. [265]

### Anti static plastic
Plastic can be cleaned and made anti-static by wiping down with a solution of 1 tablespoon of distilled vinegar to 1 gallon of water. This will cut down on the plastics' tendency to attract dust. [266]

### Bath tub film
Bath tub film can be removed by wiping with vinegar and then with soda. Rinse clean with water.[267]

### Blanket renewal
Cotton and wool blankets become soft, fluffy and free of soap odor if 2 cups of distilled vinegar are added to the rinse cycle of the wash.[268]

### Bottle cleaning
Unsightly film in small-necked bottles and other containers can be cleaned by pouring vinegar into the bottle and shaking. For tougher stains, add a few tablespoons of rice or sand and shake vigorously. Rinse thoroughly and repeat until clean or determined hopeless.[269]

### Brass polish
Brass, copper and pewter will shine if cleaned with the following mixture. Dissolve 1 teaspoon of salt in 1 cup of distilled vinegar and stir in flour until it becomes a paste. Apply paste to the metals and let it stand for about 15 minutes. Then rinse with clean warm water and polish until dry.[270]

### Brighten the light
Gasoline and propane lantern mantles last longer and burn brighter on the same amount of fuel if they are soaked for several hours in distilled vinegar and allowed to dry before using.[271]

### Carpet renewal
The colors in carpets and rugs will often look like they have taken a new lease on life if they are brushed with a mixture of 1 cup of vinegar in a gallon of water.[272]

### Carpet stain removal
A mixture of one teaspoon of liquid detergent and 1 teaspoon of distilled vinegar in a pint of lukewarm water will remove non-oily stains from carpets. Apply it to the stain with a soft brush or

towel and rub gently. Rinse with a towel moistened with clean
water and blot dry. Repeat this procedure until the stain is gone.
Then dry quickly, using a fan or hair dryer. This should be done
as soon as the stain is discovered.[273]

### Catsup stains
Spots caused by catsup can be removed from 100 percent
cotton, cotton polyester and permanent press fabrics if they are
sponged with distilled vinegar within 24 hours and washed
immediately.[274]

### Chrome and stainless steel polish
Chrome and stainless steel can be polished by wiping with
distilled vinegar.[275]

### Clean dishwasher
1/2 cup of distilled vinegar added to the rinse cycle of automatic
dishwashers will help keep the drain line clean and odorless.[276]

### Clogged drain
A clogged drain may sometimes be opened by pouring in a
handful of baking soda, followed by a half cup of vinegar,down
the drain pipe.[277]

### Clothes washing magic
Clothes will rinse better if a cup of white vinegar is added to the
last rinse water. The acid in vinegar is too mild to harm fabrics
but strong enough to dissolve the alkalies in soaps and
detergents.[278]

### Coffee maker cleaner (automatic)
Vinegar can help to dissolve mineral deposits that collect in
automatic drip coffee makers from hard water. Fill the reservoir
with vinegar and run it through a brewing cycle. Rinse
thoroughly with water when the cycle is finished. ( Be sure sure
to check the owners manual for specific instructions.)

## Coffee maker cleaner (percolator)

Stale coffee residue and oils that collect inside a percolator-type coffee maker and cause coffee to taste bitter may be removed by pouring vinegar into a cool unplugged coffee percolator. Soak overnight, rinse thoroughly and wipe with a damp cloth.

## Cola stains

Spots caused by cola-based soft drinks can be removed from 100 percent cotton, cotton polyester and permanent press fabrics if done so with in 24 hours. To do it, sponge distilled vinegar directly onto the stain and rub away the spots. Then clean according to the directions on the manufacturer's care tag.[279]

## Cooking odors

To eliminate unpleasant cooking odors, boil a teaspoon of distilled vinegar in a cup of water.in the room with the unwanted odor.[280]

## Cut Flower preserver

Fresh cut flowers can be kept blooming longer by adding two tablespoons of vinegar, plus three tablespoons of sugar to each quart of warm water. The stems must be kept in three to four inches of the nutrient.[281]

## Cutting grease

A few teaspoons of distilled or spirit vinegar will help to cut the grease.[282]

## Decal removal

Old decals can be easily removed by sponging on distilled vinegar. Allow the vinegar to soak in for a few minutes and then wash off.[283]

## Deodorant stains

Deodorant and anti-perspirants stains may be removed from clothing by lightly rubbing with distilled vinegar and laundering as usual.[284]

## Deodorizing containers

The odors of the former contents of old jars and other containers may be removed by rinsing them in white vinegar.[285]

## Dish washing magic

Chalky deposits are often left on dinnerware washed in dishwashers. To remove the deposits, place the affected pieces in the dishwasher. Put a cup filled with vinegar on the bottom rack and run the machine for five minutes. Stop the machine and refill the cup, whose contents have been replaced with water, with vinegar. Repeat this cycle and follow by a complete cycle with dishwasher detergent.[286]

## Doggie did it on the carpet

Test the color fastness of the carpet with vinegar in an inconspicuous place. Then sprinkle distilled vinegar over the fresh doggie accident. Wait a few minutes and sponge from the center outward. Blot up with a dry cloth. This procedure may need to be repeated for stubborn stains.[287]

## Dust reducer

Sponging away grease and dirt with a sponge dipped in distilled vinegar will keep exhaust fan grills, air-conditioner blades and grills dust free.[288]

## Dyeing mordant

When dyeing fabric, add a cup full of distilled vinegar to the last rinse to set the color. [289]

## Electric irons

To remove burn stains from an electric iron, mix 1 part salt with 1 part vinegar and heat in a small aluminum pan. Use this mix to polish the iron as you would silver.[290]

## Fish bowl cleaner

Eliminate that ugly deposit in the gold fish tank by rubbing it with a cloth dipped in vinegar and rinsing well[291].

## Fresh bread box
After cleaning the bread box, keep it smelling sweet by wiping it down with a cloth moistened in distilled vinegar.[292]

## Fresh lunch box
It is easy to take out the heavy stale smell often found in lunch boxes. Dampen a piece of fresh bread with distilled vinegar and leave it in the lunch box overnight.[293]

## Freshen baby clothes
The addition of 1 cup of distilled vinegar to each load of baby clothes during the rinse cycle will naturally break down uric acid and soapy residue leaving the clothes soft and fresh.[294]

## Fruit stains
To eliminate fruit stains from your hands, rub your hands with a little distilled vinegar and wipe them with a cloth.[295]

## Garbage disposal cleaner
Garbage disposals may be kept clean and odor free with vinegar cubes. Vinegar cubes are made by filling an ice tray with a mixture of 1 cup of vinegar and enough water to fill the ice tray and freezing it. Run the mixture through the disposal, then flush it with cold water for a minute or so.[296]

## Grass killer
Unwanted grass can be eliminated from sidewalks and driveways by pouring distilled vinegar on it.[297]

## Hole removal
After a hem or seam is removed, there are often unsightly holes left in the fabric. These holes can be removed by placing a cloth, moistened with distilled vinegar, under the fabric and ironing.[298]

## Keeping colors fast
To hold colors in fabrics which tend to run, soak them for a few minutes in distilled vinegar before washing. [299]

## Leather cleaning

Leather articles can be cleaned with a mixture of distilled vinegar and linseed oil. Rub the mixture into the leather and then polish with a soft cloth.[300]

## Lime fighter

Lime used for gardening can be easily washed off of the hands with vinegar. Follow the washing with a thorough rinsing in cold water and an application of a good skin lotion.[301]

## Loosen joints

To loosen old glue around rungs and joints of tables and chairs under repair, apply distilled vinegar with a small oil can.[302]

## No-frost windshields

Distilled vinegar will help to keep frost off of the windshields. A solution of 3 parts vinegar to 1 part water wiped on the windshield should do the trick.[303]

## Nylon hose preserver

Nylon hose will look better and last longer if 1 tablespoon of vinegar is added to the rinse water when washing.[304]

## Onion odor removal

To quickly remove the odor of onions from your hands, rub your hands with distilled vinegar.[305]

## Oven grease retardant

Grease buildup in an oven can be prevented by wiping with a cleaning rag that has been moistened in distilled vinegar and water.[306]

## Paint brush softener

Soak the paint brush in hot vinegar, then wash out with warm, sudsy water.[307]

## Patent leather shiner
Patent leather will shine better if wiped with a soft cloth which has been moisten with distilled vinegar.[308]

## Removing smokey odors from clothes
Smoky odors may be removed from clothes by hanging them over a steaming bath to which one cup of distilled vinegar has been added.[309]

## Removing stains
A mixture of salt and vinegar will clean coffee and tea stains from chinaware.[310]

## Room odors
To remove odors from a room, place a small bowl of distilled vinegar in the warmest corner of the room. Even the odors of fresh paint or stale tobacco may be removed in this manner.[311]

## Rust cutter
A rusted or corroded bolt may be loosened by soaking it in distilled vinegar.[312]

## Scenting a room
To add a pleasant scent to a room while at the same time removing an unpleasant odor, add cardamom or other fragrant spice to a bowl of distilled vinegar and place in the warmest corner of the room.[313]

## Sharp knit fabric creases
To obtain a sharper crease in your knit fabrics, dampen them with a cloth wrung out from a solution of 1/3 distilled vinegar and 2/3 water. Place a brown paper bag over the crease and iron.[314]

## Shine stainless steel
Remove those unsightly spots on your stainless steel by rubbing the spots with a cloth that has been dampened with vinegar.[315]

## Shining formica counters

Formica tops and counters will shine if cleaned with a cloth soaked in distilled vinegar.[316]

## Shining no-wax linoleum

No-wax linoleum will shine better if wiped with a solution of 1/2 cup of white vinegar in 1/2 gallon of water.[317]

## Sparkling glassware

One-half cup of distilled vinegar added to a gallon of rinse water will remove soap film from glassware and make it shine.[318]

## Sparkling plumbing fixtures

Soap and stain build up can be removed from chrome and plastic fixtures if they are cleaned with a mixture of 1 teaspoon of salt and 2 tablespoons of distilled vinegar.[319]

## Stubborn stain of pots 'n pans

Soak the pots and pans in full-strength distilled vinegar for 30 minutes, then wash in hot, soapy water.[320]

## Suds Killer

Excess laundry suds that develop during hand laundry may be eliminated by splashing a little vinegar into the second rinse. Follow this with another rinse in plain water.[321]

## Tea kettle deposits

Over a period of time , depending on the water supply, lime deposits will form in a tea kettle. The deposits may be removed by gently boiling a 1/2 cup of vinegar in the tea pot which has been filled with water.[322]

## Toilet bowl cleaner

Stubborn stains can be removed from the toilet by spraying them with vinegar and brushing vigorously. The bowl may be deodorized by adding 3 cups of distilled vinegar. Allow it to remain for a half hour, then flush.[323]

## Tough stains
Stains on hard-to-clean glass, aluminum, or porcelain utensils may be loosened by boiling in a solution of one part vinegar to eight parts water. The utensils should then be washed in hot soapy water.[324]

## Unclog the showerhead
Corrosion may be removed from showerheads or faucets by soaking them in diluted distilled vinegar overnight. This may be easily accomplished by saturating a terry cloth towel in vinegar and wrapping it around the showerhead or faucet.[325]

## Varnished wood renewal
Varnished wood often takes on a cloudy appearance. If the cloudiness hasn't gone through to the wood, the cloudiness can be removed by rubbing the wood with a soft lintless cloth wrung out from a solution of 1 tablespoon of distilled vinegar in a quart of luke-warm water. Complete the job by wiping the surface with a soft dry cloth.[326]

## Washing the woodwork
Dirt and grime can be easily removed from woodwork with a solution of 1 cup of ammonia, 1/2 cup of distilled vinegar, and 1/4 cup of baking soda in a cup of warm water. This solution will not dull the finish or leave streaks.[327]

## Water or alcohol marks on wood
Stubborn rings resulting from wet glasses being placed on wood furniture may be removed by rubbing with a mixture of equal parts of distilled vinegar and olive oil. Rub with the grain and polish for the best results.[328]

## Window washing magic
Make a solution of 1 part warm water and 1 part distilled vinegar. Wash the windows with this and dry with a soft cloth. This should produce shining, streakless windows. Dried paint on windows is removed with hot vinegar..[329]

## Wine stains

Spots caused by wine can be removed from 100 percent cotton, cotton polyester and permanent press fabrics if done so within 24 hours. To do it, sponge distilled vinegar directly onto the stain and rub away the spots. Then clean according to the directions on the manufacturer's care tag.[330]

## Wood paneling cleaner

Wood paneling may be cleaned with a mixture of 1 ounce of olive oil and 2 ounces of distilled vinegar in 1 quart of warm water. Moisten a soft cloth with the solution and wipe the paneling. The yellowing is then removed by wiping with a soft, dry cloth.[331]

# CHAPTER 13

## POP AND SUPERSTITION

While researching vinegar many pieces of trivia surfaced. Some of it is interesting but of no particular use. Some of it is a bit difficult to believe, some of it impossible to believe and some of it so unbelievable as to be humorous. It is included here for those interested in such trivia.

One of the more bizarre uses of vinegar is found in the Soviet Union. Some people there use something called vinegar essence to commit suicide. It is 80 percent acetic acid, and is normally used in food processing.

According to the "Soviet Encyclopedia," this type of poisoning is one of the most frequent types of domestic poisonings and is usually the result of a suicide attempt. A dose of 30 to 50 milliliters is often all that is required.

It is a gruesome way to go, however. It causes severe burns on all parts of the mouth, throat and stomach. The blood floods into the intestines, blood cells are destroyed and the victim goes into shock.

It is also rather reliable. Only immediate hospitalization can give the victim a slight chance of survival once ingestion has occurred.

Just for the record, it would take quite a bit of household-strength vinegar to produce these results. The person would most likely pass out before a fatal amount of normal strength vinegar could be consumed.

*

In many cultures, vinegar symbolizes bitterness and misfortune.

*

It is a Chinese life emblem.[332]

*

If one dreams about vinegar, it signifies jealousy or a quarrel.

*

It is best to make vinegar in the moon light[333].

*

Tap a barrel full of wine when the moon rises in March and it will turn into vinegar.[334]

*

If someone enters while you are making wine you must say "Santo Martino" or the bad eye will turn the wine into vinegar.[335]

*

If cider is put into a vat to cure and the moon is not full , the cider will turn into vinegar.[336]

*

Going near a vinegar barrel is bad luck. [337]

*

Spilling vinegar on the floor is bad luck. [338]

*

A barrel of vinegar touched by a woman during her menstrual period will spoil. [339]

*

If a woman goes near cider while on her menstrual period, the vinegar made from it will not be good.[340]

*

Food pickled or canned with vinegar by a woman on her menstrual period will spoil.[341]

*

If you write the name of a "hard " woman on a piece of heavy brown paper and put it into the in the ferment, it will make a good vinegar.[342]

*

If you throw away a vinegar mother, you will never be able to make vinegar. You must save it or give it away.[343]

*

Never give vinegar away or your luck will go with it.[344]

## MISCELLANEOUS VINEGAR QUOTES

Vinegar, the son of wine.
    Babylonian Talmud: Baba Metzia[345]

One Rich drop of honey sweet,
As an alluring luscious treat,
Is known to tempt more flies, by far,
Than a whole tun of vinegar.
            William Comb, *Dr. Syntax in search*
                *of a wife*[346]

A loaf of bread the Walrus said,
Is what we chiefly need:
Pepper and vinegar besides
Are very good indeed
Now if you're ready, Oysters dear,
We can begin to feed.
            Lewis Carrol 1932-1898[347]

Vinegar in hand is better than Havla to come
            Persian Proverb[348]

A poet that fails in writing becomes often a morose critic; the
weak and insipid white wine makes at length an excellent
vinegar.
        William Shenstone, Essays: On writing and Books[349]

'Tis melancholy, and a fearful sign
Of human frailty, folly, also crime,
That love and marriage rarely can combine,
Although they both are born in the same climb,
Marriage from love, like vinegar from wine-
A sad, sour, sober beverage- by time
Is sharpened by its celestial flavour,
Down to a celestial household savour.
                              Lord Byron
                              1778-1824 [350]

Of such vinegar aspect
That they'll not show their teeth by way of smile
Though Nestor swear the jest be laughable
                    William Shakespear
                    The Merchant of Venice
                    Act 1 Scene 1[351]

Wit, like tierce claret, when 't begans to pall,
Neglected and 's of no use at all,
But in its full perfection of decay,
Turns vinegar, and comes again in play
                    Charles Sackville,
                    To Mr. Edward Howard [352]

Much vinegar makes the wine cheap
                    Jewish proverb[353]

Mayest thou have neither salt nor vinegar in thy house.
                    Jewish proverb (curse?)[354]

Pour vinegar and oil into the same cruse and thou wilt say
that, as foes, they keep asunder.
          Aeschylus, Agamemnon (458 BC)[355]

The bitterer the salad of endives, the stronger must be the vinegar.
Palestinian Proverb[356]

Our Garrick's a salad; for in him we see
Oil, vinegar, sugar and saltiness agree.
Oliver Goldsmith 1730-1774[357]

Love matches are made by people who are content, for a mouth full of honey, to condemn themselves to a of vinegar.
Countess of Blessington,
The Commonplace Book[358]

Beware of vinegar of sweete wine, and the anger of a peaceable man.
John Florio, First Fruits 1578[359]

You drink vinegar when you have wine at your elbow.
Thomas Fuller, Gnomologia[360]

Acetobacters, the vinegar producing bacteria, drink a lot of alcohol and excrete vinegar. Aside from this ,they are much different from alcoholics.
The Vinegar Man

Sour makes sweet happen.
The Vinegar Man

# VINEGAR IN OTHER LANGUAGES

Arabic[361] ..................................................... chall
Bantu ........................................... wayini w samuka
Chinese........................................................ tsù
Czechoslovakian[362]........................................ocet
Danish[363]................................................... eddike
Dutch[364]..................................................... azjin
Esperanto[365] .............................................vinagro
Finnish[366].................................................etikka
French.................................................... vinaigre
German.....................................................essig
Greek[367].................................................... xi'di
Hausa...........................................ruwan tsami yami
Hebrew[368] ............................................... chomets
Hindi.................................................... toori
Hungarian[369] ............................................... ecet
Italian .....................................................aceto
Japanese...................................................... su
Norwegian[370]............................................. eddik
Polish[371] .................................................ocet
Rumanian[372]............................................... otet
Russian[373] ..............................................úksus
Serbo Croatian[374]............................................ocat
Spanish[375] .................................................vinagre
Swahili[376]................................................. siki
Swedish[377]............................................... ättika
Tagalog...................................................... suka
Turkish[378]...............................................sirke
Xousa.......................................................iviniga
Yiddish[379].................................................essig
Zulu........................................................uvinika

# ALCHEMIC SYMBOLS

---

## JAPANESE SCRIPT (KANJI)

BITTER      SAKE

### EGYPTIAN

| EARLY SCRIPT | MODERN SCRIPT |
|---|---|
| PRONOUNCED<br>"HUM'TCHA" | COPT |

## HEBREW
חֹמֶץ

# CHAPTER 14

## VINEGAR AS A HOBBY

After reading this book, you will posses a wealth of knowledge about vinegar. You will be a vinegar connoisseur. This will put you in a unique position to use and enjoy it in many ways. Anyone can enjoy hours of pleasure from taking up vinegar as a hobby. Because vinegar is so useful in so many ways, the benefits of becoming a vinegarologist is limited only by time and the imagination. In this section we will discuss some of the ways in which you may enjoy vinegar as a hobby.

## VINEGAR HISTORIAN

Having purchased and read this book, you already know more than most people about vinegar. This makes you something of a vinegar historian already. With all of the references listed in this book and all of the resources you will discover once you begin to look, researching vinegar can be a rewarding challenge. Areas of specialization could include:

> Collecting vinegar patents from around the world
> Collecting quotes on vinegar
> Vinegar trivia
> Novel ways in which vinegar is used
> Recipes in which vinegar is used
> > vinaigrettes
> > barbecue sauces using vinegar
> > unusual vinegar recipes
> Vinegars historical use

The list could go on but these can get you started. A vinegar historian will have an interesting story to tell at the beginning and end of every salad.

## COLLECTING, AGING AND INVESTING IN VINEGARS

The easiest way to enjoy vinegar is to collect it. There are many kinds of vinegars, made from many different things, from many different places and made by many different processes. Any of them will possess some unique characteristics that could make it a collector's items. You will not need any special tools or equipment, and the investment can be easily tailored to your budget. Your knowledge, judgment, taste and nose are the most essential ingredient to making you a good collector.

All you do is exercise you best judgement in selecting the best vinegars you can afford. If you find a particularly good one, buy a few bottles label them with pertinate information (see labeling) and store them away to age.

Of course a cellar, an electronic ph indicator, a thermometer and other testing equipment could be useful and could add to the image of one who really knows his vinegars, but they are not absolutely necessary. Unlike some wines, vinegar is relatively stable and requires a minimum of care as long as some basic guidelines are followed.

### Investment
Vinegar is the result of refining the alcoholic product from which it was made. Vinegars, which are aged, increase even more in intrinsic value. And though they may not increase as fast as wines and other alcohols, the risk of spoilage is significantly less. It does not require terribly special conditions for storage. It, like gold, has many uses and therefore will be of some value no matter what political, economic or religious changes take place. For these reasons vinegar has good investment value.

## VINEGAR  TASTING

Many people have heard of wine tasting, but not many know that there is such a thing as vinegar tasting. Still fewer know that there are contests in which superior vinegars compete for honors just as the wines and other spirits compete.

You will need a wide mouthed glass of from 4 to 6 ounces to pour the vinegar into. You will not be using this much vinegar. But you will need to be able to stick a couple of fingers holding a sugar cube down into the glass, so the glass must be the proper shape and size to accommodate this maneuver.

The vinegar to be tasted should be at room temperature. It should be left in its container until it is time to be tasted. Any literature or other presentation about it should be made available to the tasters, unless it is a blind taste test. Additionally you should have a list of the vinegars being tested, some score sheets ( see suggested sample in appendix ) and some certificates ribbons or other awards for the winners if it is a contest (The awards are optional, but add a nice touch).

If the event is a contest, all of the criteria should be spelled out clearly. All of the materials should be laid out in an orderly arrangement and explanations given as to how the event is to proceed.

You will also need some rectangular, Domino brand, sugar cubes. Some water to wash out the mouth is also useful.

One of the foremost authorities on the subject of vinegar tasting, Dante Bagnani, of American Foods. Born the son of a vinegar maker, Mr. Bagnani has been around vinegar all of his long life. He is not only knowledgeable about the making of vinegar, but he is a true connoisseur.

He explained the art of vinegar tasting.

"In tasting vinegars, we use the same methods , up to a point that we use in tasting wines. First is the visual, where we look for clarity, brilliance and characteristic color. If it is murky or cloudy we would stop right there.(The vinegar would be disqualified from further consideration.) So it has to be clean looking, no murkiness and no sediment and proper color characteristics. The white wine vinegars may be pale or slightly chardoney."

{Authors Note}These attributes are more critical in commercial vinegars than homemade ones. And even some very good commercial vinegars are still cloudy because they are live culture vinegars and their cloudiness is a kind of hallmark. Balsamics and other dark vinegars also often lack clarity and brilliance. These vinegars should be judged in a class by themselves.

"Now the aroma and bouquet. The aroma comes from the grapes (or other fruits) that the vinegar was made from. The bouquet comes later from the barrel where it develops. Now we've got to be careful in putting our nose in the glass. With wine you can sniff all you want, but the acetic acid in vinegar will throw your head back. First swirl it around in the glass to break up the esters, then pass it quickly under the nose to get the aroma. You are looking for cleanliness, no mustiness, no off smells like mildew. If there were a bad smell coming from it , again you would stop right there (The vinegar would be disqualified from further consideration).

"Smelling the vinegar is very important because it helps to prepare you for the full experience of the vinegar.

"Now we go for the taste. As you know the taste buds are what take the various tastes of sour, sweet, bitter, salty and hot and send them on to the brain. ( Any other taste sensations are picked up in the nose. This is very important to remember when evaluating vinegar. If you have a bad cold, for example, you may only be able to pick up the sourness of vinegar and miss its subtleties altogether). The taste buds which pick up the sour taste are on the sides of the tongue.

"In Paris , where they have an annual wine vinegar tasting, they found when tasting vinegar, you will taste the first one, but then the taste buds close up because of the acid. And you have to wait 10 or 15 minutes until they open up again before you can taste another one. Now with the sugar cube, we soak it in the vinegar, let it soak up the vinegar and then suck the vinegar out of the sugar cube. That fools the taste buds and they stay open and the sugar does not change the flavor whatsoever. You can get all of the nuances, complexities, all of the various things that you want to get (see Taste Descriptors appendix).

"After you have tasted it, you can spit it out or swallow it. Rinse out the mouth and then start all over again with the next vinegar."

Another way to conduct a less formal vinegar tasting is to use mayonnaise. Prepare a tasting dip.(see Food Uses section). Then set out salt-free crackers or bread sticks or even celery or other bland vegetables. Label the dips well. Pass out comment slips or score sheets for each of the guest. Tabulate the scores or review the comments at the end of the party or in a follow up form letter to all of the guests.

## VINEGAR TASTING PARTIES

As a vinegar connoisseur you will want to sponsor vinegar tasting parties. These parties often bring together some of the more interesting people in the human race. But just as important they bring together some of the most interesting vinegars in the world along with some of the most interesting foods prepared from vinegar. Imagine a party with twenty or more different kinds of vinegar, vinegar pie, vinegar cake, vinegar cheese, home made mustards and sauces of every description and the list goes on. Just call up some friends and tell them they are invited to a vinegar tasting party. Have them bring a special kind of vinegar and prepare one dish of their choice using vinegar. Now you gotta admit you don't go to a party like this every week-end."

## VINEGAR CONTESTS

Another interesting way to enjoy vinegar is to put on contests to compare the qualities of various home made vinegars, much the same as they do already with pies, cakes, chili and gumbo. This can be particularly interesting and exciting for church groups or social clubs.who are seeking new activities to interest their members. Wine making clubs may also want to sponsor some vinegar making contest.

These contests may be general in nature, that is to say, they can combine all of the vinegars together and look for specific characteristics or they may divide the vinegars into categories if there are enough entries. The criteria such as upper and lower limits of the percentage of acetic acid must be set by the sponsoring group. It is important to clearly explain the categories and criteria so as to avoid any misunderstandings.

Awards can be given for each element, category or overall quality. Certificates may be inexpensively printed or plaques or trophies can be ordered from companies who make such items for sports events.

## BLENDING VINEGAR

Another way to enjoy vinegar as a connoisseur is to engage in the art of blending. The vinegar industry, like the wine industry, blends its products when the qualities it wants are found in two or more products. On the home level this can be an exciting and rewarding skill to acquire. With so many vinegars available, the possibilities of new blended vinegars are staggering.

Studying wines and the ideas used for blending them will prove instructive. Talking to others engaged in the same hobby is also useful. If you do not know anyone, convert someone. Two heads are better than one , even if one is a goat head[380]. See vinegar making section for more information.

## MAKING VINEGAR FROM ALCOHOL

If you are ready for the challenge of making vinegar, a good place to start is making it from alcohol. From this stage you are able to make vinegar from a large variety of alcohols. The important things to watch for here are chemicals which are used to prevent the alcohols from turning to vinegar and alcohol dilutions which are too high or too low (see vinegar making section for details).

This level of the hobby is very good for the home cook who wants to add something special to his bag of tricks. But it will be of special interest to the professional chef who wants to add a "mysteriously unduplicatable" touch to his reputation.

## MAKING VINEGAR FROM "SCRATCH"

For the serious and adventurous connoisseur nothing measures up to the rewards of the challenge of creating vinegar from raw materials. Depending on the level of involvement, the investment in equipment is not terribly great. It does require study and practice to become skilled, but the rewards are well worth it. The magic of triple fermentation can only be appreciated thru participation in the experience. If you become skilled at making vinegar from scratch, you will have joined a select group of people who are as unique as the product they create.

# APPENDICES

# RAW MATERIALS APPENDIX

## PREPARATION OF FRESH FRUITS FOR VINEGAR MANUFACTURE

The process used in extracting fruit juices for vinegar making depend upon the nature of the fruit. Some fruits give considerably more juice if they are crushed and allowed to undergo a preliminary alcoholic fermentation for a few days before pressing the juice from the pulp. Apricots, bananas, pears, peaches, fresh prunes, plums and other pulpy fruits are usually handled in this manner.[381] On the other hand, apples, grapes, oranges and other fruits that do not contain significant amounts of pulp are usually crushed and pressed without undergoing that process.

A word of caution about the preparation of fruit juices for making vinegar. Many fruits are periodically sprayed with various poisonous chemicals, insecticides and fungicides to increase yields, extend shelf life and improve marketability. Unless the vinegar maker is careful, some of these poisonous materials may end up in the final vinegar product,

The amount of arsenic contaminating the juice is affected by the number of arsenical sprays applied and the time between the last spray and harvesting. The fruit should be washed in a 0.3 to 1.3 percent solution of hydrochloric acid before crushing if there is any chance that the maximum limits of arsenic trioxide may be exceeded in the completed vinegar.

This problem is usually found in apples, but other fruits like peaches and grapes,for example, may also be dangerous in this respect.

## Apples
Most apples contain enough sugar to make a vinegar of 4.5 percent or more acetic acid content.[382]. Winter apples have the highest sugar content, while summer apples have the lowest.

For that reason summer apples are not recommended for vinegar making.The apples do not have to be the best of quality, but care should be taken to remove any defects such as mold or mildew that would impart a bad taste or odor. Incidentally, apple scraps such as the cores and peels are often used to make rather good vinegar. Green (unripened) apples don't work too well because much of their starch has not been converted into sugar.

Contrary to popular belief, sweet apples do not necessarily contain more sugar than sour ones. In fact, some "sweet" varieties contain less sugar. That is because the sweet taste of some of the sweet apples is due to the absence of malic acid rather than the abundance of sugar.

Apples are grated and pressed as if you were preparing cider. A household juicer will also do a great job for small-scale production. A hammer mill type of grinder for whole apples and an apple grater for recovering the juice retained in the pomace is better for larger productions.[383]

While preliminary fermentation between grinding and pressing is not common in the manufacture of cider vinegar, it seems that larger yields are obtained by using this procedure. Ten to 20 gallons of actively fermenting cider are added and mixed with the pomace to facilitate yeast fermentation and to prevent premature acetification. The mixture is pressed after being allowed to ferment for two or three days.

The main disadvantage in this procedure, in addition to the extra processing costs involved, is the danger of premature acetification as a result of early contamination by acetic acid bacteria. This frequently halts alcoholic fermentation and results in a partially fermented vinegar of inferior quality.

Dried apple chops and the dried cores and parings from apple canning factories and apple drying companies are sometimes used in the commercial production of vinegar[384]. By rehydrating this material, a sweet solution is produced from which vinegar is made. If the original material used for this purpose is clean and sound, vinegar of reasonable quality can be produced.

But this vinegar cannot be legally called cider vinegar because it does not come from the liquid taken directly from apples.

### Bananas
Ripe bananas contain about 17 percent of fermentable sugars. The fruit is crushed and water is added to make the mixture fluid enough for fermentation. When alcoholic fermentation is complete, the mash is filtered and the liquid that remains is then distilled. The distillate is then acidified, creating a vinegar that possesses an aroma similar to fresh bananas[385]

Many other tropical fruits may be used to make vinegar.[386]

### Berries
Vinegar produced from raspberries, blueberries and other berries are very good. Vinegar made from red raspberries will keep the flavor and aroma of the fruit indefinitely. This quality makes it very good for flavoring food. Vinegar made from berries will be naturally dark in color, but it can easily be cleared

### Grapes
Some of the best vinegar possible can be made from grapes (*Vitis vinifera)*. White or red grapes from Europe and the Western United States are at the top of this list. Grapes contain much more sugar than apples and so a stronger vinegar can be made. One hundred and fifty gallons of grape juice will yield about 135 gallons of 9.8 percent vinegar in the laboratory. In the home one could expect about a 6.6 percent acetic acid content. The chief drawback is their cost.[387]

Lacking the access to the grapes, it is possible to make a rather good vinegar for home use from store bought grape juice. It is very important to obtain juice that has no additives and is full-strength. This will most likely be a concord grape juice, but a little shopping in the juice section of the supermarket or the health food store may produce some interesting options.

## Oranges
The Bureau of Chemistry of the United States Department of Agriculture has shown that a very acceptable vinegar can be made from oranges, either on a household or on a commercial scale. Cull oranges will result in a vinegar which is not only equal to the best grade of vinegar but in some markets can be made commercially competitive with apple vinegar.[388]

At one time in California cull oranges were used to make vinegar on a large scale[389], The juice was squeezed in large fluted bronze rolls. The fresh juice containing the orange oil from the skins was centrifuged to separate and recover the oil, and the juice was then used for vinegar making.

For home use, orange juice from concentrates should be used because fresh orange juice contains many oils that become bitter when made into vinegar.

## Papaya
The wine made from papaya will need to be aerated in order to make vinegar from it, otherwise it will not acidify. The submerged system using wood shavings have shown the best results. Nutrients are needed to get the culture going, but these nutrients do not seem to affect the rate of acetification. [390]

## Peaches
Although the average sugar content of peaches is a bit lower than that of apples, some varieties contain enough sugar to make vinegar. Juicy varieties of the Carman type are best suited for this purpose. If possible, the peaches should be allowed to ripen on the tree, since tree-ripened peaches seem to always contain more sugar than those picked while green and allowed to ripen during shipment or storage. Peach juice ferments easily and good, flavorful vinegar can often be made from peaches that would otherwise rot.

## Pears
Pears may be used for making vinegar. Even varieties like the

Kieffer, which is low in sugar may be made to produce a satisfactory vinegar if well-ripened. [391]

## Persimmons

Persimmons grow almost everywhere in the United States. Those grown in the Southern states, tend to be the richest in sugar. Experiments conducted by the Bureau of Chemistry, United States Department of Agriculture, show that they can be used for making vinegar[392]. Fruits like persimmons and figs, which possess a high-sugar and low-moisture content, must be diluted to have the correct concentration of sugar and water.

# SYRUPS

## Honey vinegar

Honey vinegar comes close to that made from wine or from malt.[393] The details making honey vinegar can be found in reports dating back to 1907[394] [395]. Even otherwise useless honey, like that infected by American or European foul brood, coniferous honey, honey-dew honey, honey from brood combs, or the waste from washing the extractor may be used. Some foul brood diseases are treated with sulphur drugs and these drugs may show up in the honey. Since sulphur drugs inhibit the growth of acetobacters and should not be present in food, it is always important to check any lot to be used for vinegar making for such chemicals.

## Maple Syrup Vinegar

Maple syrup or maple syrup skimmings that have been burned may be used for vinegar making. Since maple products contain concentrations of sugar that are too high for fermentation to take place, they must be diluted until they contain no more than about 13 per cent sugar.

## Whey Vinegar

Milk sugar in the form of whey is obtained as a by-product in the manufacture of certain kinds of cheese. The sugar in this case is lactose, and this may also be fermented to alcohol and then to vinegar.[396]. It is very difficult to eliminate undesirable flavors due to milk serum proteins in vinegar made from this material. Whey contains only four to five per cent fermentable sugar in the form of lactose. So whey used for vinegar manufacture must be concentrated.[397] Whey vinegar has a light brown appearance similar to malt vinegar and an aroma slightly suggestive of whey. It often has a salty taste which is not considered universally objectionable.

The following is a list of a few of the materials which have been used as vinegar bases.

| | |
|---|---|
| APPLES | MANGOES |
| APRICOTS | MILK |
| BARLEY | MOLLASSES |
| BEETS | ORANGES |
| BERRIES | PEARS |
| CANE | PERSIMMONS |
| CHERRIES | PINEAPPLES |
| COCONUT | PLUMS |
| CORN | POTATOES |
| DATES | RAISINS |
| FIGS | RICE |
| GRAPES | WOOD |
| HONEY | |

# WOODS FOR AGING VINEGAR

The contribution of wood to the final flavor of vinegar is significant if the vinegar is either fermented slowly or aged for an extended period of time. There are many woods that will contribute to the complexities of fine vinegars. A few of them are listed here.

By far the most popular wood is oak. These include the following kinds of oak

white oak  +
red oak  +
chestnut oak  +
French oak  +
Other European oaks  +

Other woods which have been used are;

*Albizzia odratissima*   Ceylon, Burma
bald cypress  USA
basswood  USA
beech  USA  +
black cherry  USA
chestnut  Europe
*Cryptomeria*  Japan
elm  USA
larch  Europe
mulberry  Europe  +
pine  Europe
red gum  USA
She oak..Australia (*Casuarina fraseriana*)
sugar maple  USA
sycamore  USA
white ash  USA
yellow birch  USA

---

**WOODS RECOMMENDED FOR BALSAMIC**
**VINEGAR**
ash
cherry
chestnut
juniper
mulberry
Oak
Slovanian oak

---

Woods, like other materials, must be selected with care. They can add to a product or make it undesirable. A thorough discussion of this subject may be found in the paper Some Aspects of the Wood Container as a Factor in Wine Maturation by V.L. Singleton. Available at the University of California Davis California.

+ = RECOMMENDED

# VINEGAR FLAVORING MATERIALS APPENDIX

Vinegar may be flavored with many different materials. This appendix lists a few formulas which have produced outstanding vinegars. Additionally it contains a list of materials which have been used for flavoring vinegars.

The proportions given here are for distilled or white wine vinegars, but any other unflavored vinegars may be used. The formulas should be used as guidelines to give you an idea of the ratios. Experimentation pays dividends.

Basil
1 ounce per quart of vinegar

Cayenne pepper
1/2 ounce per quart of vinegar

Chili
4 bay leaves
6 dried hot chili peppers
4 large garlic cloves
1 quart of vinegar

Curry powder
3 ounces per quart of vinegar

Dill (fresh)
7 sprigs per quart of vinegar

Garlic
8 cloves (2 ounces) per quart of vinegar

Marjoram
7 sprigs per quart of vinegar

Mint
1 1/2 cups mint (fresh / crushed)

1 cup of sugar
1 quart white wine or cider vinegar

Roses
3 ounces of red rose petals per quart of white wine vinegar or rice vinegar

Shallots
4 ounces per quart of vinegar

Tarragon
2 ounces per quart of vinegar

## SPICE LIST

Absinthe
Allspice
Basil
Cardamom
Cayenne
Celery seeds
Celery
Cheveril
Chives
Cinnamon
Cloves
Dill
Fennel
Ginger
Kumquat leaves
Lavender
Lemon balm
Lemon peel

Lemon
Mace
Mint
Nasturtium
Nutmeg
Oregano
Peach blossoms
Purslane
Rosemary
Roses
Saffron
Sage
Shallots
Spearmint
Tarragon
Teas
Thyme

## TASTE DESCRIPTORS APPENDIX

In discussing the vinegars there are some descriptive terms which help to share our experiences of them. They are often referred to as descriptors. These are a few of the more common ones you are likely to hear.

# VISUAL
Presentation

| artistic | basic | unrefined |
|----------|-------|-----------|

Appearance

| brilliant<br>sedimentaceous | clear<br>various colors | cloudy<br>shiny |
|---|---|---|

# TASTE AND ODOR
Fruit

| apple<br>black current<br>fig | apricot<br>blackberry<br>grapefruit | banana<br>cherry<br>lemon |
|---|---|---|
| melon<br>pear<br>raisin<br>strawberry jam | orange<br>pineapple<br>raspberry | peach<br>prune<br>strawberry |

Spicy

| anise<br>cloves | black pepper<br>liquorice | cinnamon<br>mint |
|---|---|---|

Vegetative

| artichoke<br>black olive<br>green beans<br>stemmy | asparagus<br>eucalyptus<br>green olive<br>tea | bell pepper<br>fresh cut grass<br>hay/straw |
|---|---|---|

Earthy

| concrete | cork | dusty |
|----------|------|-------|
| moldy | mushroomy | musty |

Other

| acidy | astringent | beech |
|-------|-----------|-------|
| burnt match | burnt toast | butterscotch |
| buttery | cabbage | cardboard |
| cedar | chocolate | complex |
| delicate | filter paper | fishy |
| garlic | geranium | honey |
| horsey | jasmine | lactic acid |
| molasses | nutty | oak |
| onion | penetrating nose | pine |
| robust | rose | sauerkraut |
| skunk | smokey | soapy |
| sorbate | soy sauce | subtle |
| sulphur dioxide | sulphur | sweaty |
| sweet | vanilla | violet |
| weedy | wet dog | wet paper |
| wet wool | yeasty | |

Texture

| grainy | rough | silky |
|--------|-------|-------|
| sapid | smooth | velvety |

Bite

| harsh | mild | refined |
|-------|------|---------|

## VINEGAR COMPOSITION APPENDIX

Technically speaking, there are three types of vinegar.[398]

1. Naturally fermented vinegar; contains fermentation by products from both the alcoholic as well as the acetic fermentation.

2. Acidified-distilled vinegar; contains only those products which remain after acetification and distillation.

3. Artificial vinegars; do not have any of these important compounds.

The composition of vinegars are determined by paper-partition chromatography, ultra violet absorption spectroscopy and gas-liquid chromatography.[399]

The presence of acetoin is used to distinguish natural vinegars from artificial ones. Only cider vinegar contains malic acid. Undistilled vinegars contain a larger concentration of residual extracts than distilled vinegars.[400]

### Additives
Some substances, like salt, vitamin C, and sulphites may be added to vinegar to improve its appearance or shelf life. [401]

### Acetic acid
Acetic acid is the principle constituent in vinegar.It has a melting point of 16.7 centigrade and a boiling point of 118.0 centigrade. It will neutralize oxides and hydroxides and will decompose carbonates to produce acetate salts. It is completely miscible with water, ethanol and carbon tetrachloride but is not soluble in carbon disulfide. In a solution of water acetic acid is a weakly ionized acid $(K_a = 1.8 \times 10^{-5})$.

### Coloring agents
Coloring agents are added to improve the visual appearance of

commercial products. Caramel, cochineal, orchil and coloring agents derived from red wine which are generally used to color red wine vinegars.

## INTERNATIONAL VINEGAR SPECIFICATIONS

The World Health Organization of the United Nations, has adopted the Spanish definition of vinegar as its standard in its "codex alimentarus".

*Vinegar has to be limpid with a characteristic flavor and color, without sediments or other perceptible alterations.*

*Vinegar should contain the characteristic substances according to its origin which have not been transformed as a result of its production.*

*The total acidity calculated as acetic acid anhydride should not be less than 50 grams per liter. (these range fro 3 percent to 6 percent in other countries)The dry extracts without sugars should be not less than 10 grams per liter.Total ash content should be less than one gram per liter.The total alcohol content should not be more than 1 percent.The total residue of sulphur dioxide should not be more than 50 milligrams per kilogram.*

## LEGAL DEFINITION IN THE U. S. OF AMERICA
### ACCORDING TO FEDERAL DRUG ADMINISTRATION STANDARDS

In the United States the legal definition of vinegar is;

*1. Vinegar, cider vinegar, apple cider vinegar, is the product made by alcoholic and subsequent acetous fermentation of the juice of apples and contains in 100 cubic centimeters at 20 degrees centigrade, not less than 4 grams of acetic acid.*

*2. Wine vinegar: grape vinegar is the product made by the alcoholic and subsequent acetous fermentation of the juice of grapes and contains in 100 cubic centimeters at 20 degrees not less than 4 grams of acetic acid.*

*3. Malt vinegar is the product made by the alcoholic and subsequent acetous fermentation without distillation of an infusion of barley malt or cereals whose starch has been converted by malt and contains in 100 cubic centimeters at 20 degrees not less than 4 grams of acetic acid.*

*4. Sugar vinegar is the product made by the alcoholic and subsequent acetous fermentation of sugar syrup or refiners syrup and contains in 100 cubic centimeters at 20 degrees not less than 4 grams of acetic acid.*

*5. Glucose vinegar is the product made by the alcoholic and subsequent acetous fermentation of the solution of glucose or dextroratory and contains in 100 cubic centimeters at 20 degrees not less than 4 grams of acetic acid.*

*6. Spirit, distilled vinegar, grain vinegar is the product made by the acetous fermentation of dilute distilled alcohol and contains in 100 cubic centimeters at 20 degrees not less than 4 grams of acetic acid.*

Average Concentration of constituents in cider vinegar.

| | |
|---|---|
| Acetic acid (weight / volume)............................. | 4.94% |
| Non-Sugar Solids (w/v).................................... | 1.9% |
| Reducing sugars (w/v)..................................... | 19.6% |
| Ash (w/v)...................................................... | 0.367% |
| Alcohol (v/v)................................................ | 0.35% |
| Total solids (w/v)............................................ | 2.54% |

Note w = weight / v = volume

| | White Vinegar. | Red Vinegar. |
|---|---|---|
| Specific gravity at 15° C., . . | 1·025 | 1·012 |
| Acetic acid, per cent., . . . | 6·65 | 4·20 |
| Total solids, per cent., . . . | 2·41 | 1·12 |
| Reducing sugars, as dextrose, . . | 2·26 | 0·98 |
| Ratio, $\frac{\text{total solids}}{\text{dextrose}}$, . . . . | 1·06 | 1·14 |

| | Barley. | Rye. | Maize. | Oats. |
|---|---|---|---|---|
| | Per cent. | Per cent. | Per cent. | Per cent. |
| Moisture, . . . | 12·0 | 14·3 | 11·5 | 14·2 |
| Starch, . . . | 52·7 | 54·9 | 54·8 | 56·1 |
| Gums and sugars, . | 4·2 | 11·3 | 2·9 | 5·7 |
| Albuminoids (soluble and insoluble), . | 13·2 | 8·8 | 8·9 | 16·0 |
| Cellulose, . . . | 11·5 | 6·4 | 14·9 | 1·0 |
| Fat, . . . . | 2·6 | 2·0 | 4·7 | 4·6 |
| Ash, . . . . | 2·8 | 1·8 | 1·6 | 2·2 |
| Total, . . | 99·0 | 99·5 | 99·3 | 99·8 |

* Quoted by Nettleton, *The Manufacture of Spirit,*

# READING VINEGAR LABELS

BRAND NAME ► *Chef Luigi*

TYPE OF VINEGAR

MAKER *California Red Wine Vinegar*

*Bargetto Winery established 1933, makes Chef Luigi Red Wine Vinegar*

METHOD OF PRODUCTION
*by an old world Italian process in keeping with the Bargetto family tradition of fine wine making Chef Luigi spends two years in vats where slow wood aging assures retention of its natural wine vinegar flavor and bouquet Because of its quality and consistency, Chef Luigi has long been a favorite of gourmet chefs Made & Bottled by Bargetto's Santa Cruz Winery, Soquel, California 95073*

VINEGAR STRENGTH (GRAIN STRENGHT DIVIDED BY 10 = % ACETIC ACID)
*60 grain strength*

LOCATION OF MANUFACTURE

*Net Contents 375 ml (12 7 fl oz )* ► AMOUNT

## VINEGAR TECHNICAL DATA APPENDIX

In this appendix is found the technical reference data necessary to make, test and appreciate vinegar. This data represents many hours of work by many different scientist over many years. With humility and appreciation it is presented here.

## VINEGAR TESTING EQUIPMENT

A complete vinegar testing kit will consists a room temperature thermometer, a hydrometer assembly and a kit for testing the acetic acid concentration. A kit for testing for sulfites is also useful. Kits come with instructions for their use.

## HYDROMETER

The hydrometer is used to determine the sugar as well as the alcohol content of the soon to be vinegar stock. It is made up of three essential items. The hydrometer, a see through column to hold the liquid to be tested, and a conversion table to help you to accurately read the hydrometer. (See instructions in hydrometer kit)

## ELECTRONIC THERMOMETER

An electronic thermometer will make things go a lot faster and will reduce the chance of errors. At this writing they are not very expensive and can be found in drug and hardware stores in the United States.

## ELECTRONIC PH METER

Most of the supplies for making vinegar are rather inexpensive and can be found at the shops listed in the Suppliers of Materials appendix or in the home. The exception is the electronic PH meter. This gadget will indicate the PH of a solution rather accurately when used correctly. Some people unfamiliar with vinegar making will encourage you to "save money" by using paper strips or chemical indicators like Phenylthelene. The colors of some vinegars will stain the strips so much that it is difficult to read them reliably. Phenylthelene will work fine if your vinegar is always white, but some vinegars contain substances which will discolor the to test such a degree as to make it unreliable for the novice. The electronic PH meter one the other hand is very accurate and considerably easier to use. It has the added advantage of progressively indicating the change in PH as the test progresses. These features make it ideal for titrating.

## ACID TESTING KIT

The acid testing kit is made up of;
1) one thermometers which will measure from 30 to 110 degrees;

2) two small (about one cup each) clear vessels, one to hold the base and one to hold the acid; another small (about one cup) clear container to conduct the test in;

3) one 5 cc and one 10 cc syringe;

4) 1 quart of laboratory grade 1 normal sodium hydroxide; 1/10 normal sodium hydroxide can also be used and is recommended, for safety reasons, for the novice

5) one electronic PH meter.

The process of titrating is best explained by the seller of the kit.See titration conversion example for brief explanation

## FORMULAS AND TABLES OF CONVERSIONS

It is possible to find many recipes for making vinegar which come from other countries and other periods where different units of measurements are used. This conversion table should be of use in following those recipes.

### WEIGHTS

| | |
|---|---|
| 1 ounce | 30 grams or |
| | 6 drams |
| 1  pound | 454 grams |
| 2.2 pounds | 1 kilogram |
| 21 teaspoons / sugar | ±100 grams |

### LINEAR

| | |
|---|---|
| 1 inch | 2.54 centimeters |
| 1  meter | 39.37 inches |

### VOLUME

| | |
|---|---|
| 1  dash | 8 drops |
| 60 drops | 1 teaspoon |
| 3  teaspoon | 1 tablespoon |
| 2 tablespoons | 1 fluid ounce |
| 8 fl. ounces /16 tablespoons | 1 cup |
| 2  cups | 1 pint |
| 2 pints | 1 quart |
| 4 quarts | 1 gallon |
| 63 gallons U.S. | 1 hogshead |
| 52.5 imperial gallons | 1 hogshead |

Dry Volume ( √ Remember,dry pints and quarts are about 1/8 larger than liquid pints and quarts

| | |
|---|---|
| 2  gallons | 1 peck |
| 4 pecks | 1 bushel |

| METRIC VOLUME LIQUID | |
|---|---|
| 1 U.S. teaspoon | 5 milliliters |
| 1 U.S tablespoon | 15 milliliters |
| 1 U.S. cup | ± 237 milliliters |
| 1 U.S. pint | ±473 milliliters |
| 1 U.S. quart | 946.3 milliliters or about 1 liter |
| 1 U.S. Gallon | 3.785 liters |

| METRIC VOLUME DRY | |
|---|---|
| 1 U.S. pint | 551 liters |
| 1 U.S. quart | 1.101 liters |
| 1 U.S. peck | 8.81 liters |
| 1 U.S. bushel | 35.24 liters |

| TEMPERATURES |
|---|
| $°F = °C \times 9 \div 5 + 32$ (eg **100** °C x 9 = 900° ÷ 5 =180° + 32 = **212** °F) |
| $°C = °F - 32 \times 5 \div 9$ (eg **212** °F - 32 = 180° x 5 = 900° ÷ 9 = **100** °C) |

| **FORMULAS** |
| --- |

## ALCOHOL DILUTION FORMULA

Many times you will want to use new or left over wine, beer, whiskey or other alcohol to make vinegar. Here is a formula for calculating the amount of water and alcohol needed to arrive at the correct percentage of alcohol for vinegar making.

Multiply the number of gallons of the required mixture by the required alcohol percentage and divide the alcohol percentage of the spirits used. The quotient gives the amount of alcohol which must be used for the mixture. You may substitute cups, pints, quarts or any other measure so long as you use the same measure throughout the calculation.

### EXAMPLE

Lets suppose you are going to use a wine that was 20% alcohol. You want 100 gallons of 10% alcohol for you vinegar stock. You multiply the 100 gallons by the 10% and divide it by the 20%. This means that you will need 50 gallons of wine. The rest will be water.

Another way to arrive at this percentage is to divide the percentage of the strong spirit by the required percentage of the mixture. The quotient will give you the number of gallons of mixture which can be made with one gallon of the strong alcohol.

Using our last example, we would divide 20 by 10 and get two. This means that one gallon of 20% alcohol mixture will make 2 gallons of 10% mixture.

## TITRATION CONVERSION FORMULA

Once you have completed your titration, to determine the percentage of acetic acid your vinegar contains, you will need to use this formula to determine the percentage of acetic acid in you vinegar.

ml NAOH x n NAOH x 100 x 0.060 ÷ ml vinegar =% acetic acid

This means that;

The number of milliliters (**ml**) of sodium hydroxide (**NAOH**) multiplied by the normality (**n**) of the sodium hydroxide multiplied by **100** then multiplied again by **0.060** and then divided by the number of milliliters of vinegar (**ml vinegar**) needed to neutralize the sodium hydroxide equals the number of grams per liter of acetic acid in the solution of vinegar or the **percentage of acetic acid** in the vinegar.

### EXAMPLE

You put **30** milliliters of **.1** normal sodium hydroxide in a small container and keep adding vinegar slowly until your ph indicator says that it is neutralized. At that point you see that you have added **2** milliliters of vinegar.

Your problem would then look like this:

30 x .1 x 100 x 0.060 =18 divided by 2 = 9% acetic acid

| Media for Maintaining Cultures of Acetobacters |
|---|

Once the acetobacter has been isolated, it is necessary to have a suitable medium in which to maintain the pure culture. These culture mediums have worked very well.

Culture #1

| Combine: |
|---|
| dextrose ..................................................... 15 grams |
| yeast extract............................................... 2.5 grams |
| polypeptone................................................. 1 gram |
| |
| Then add enough water to make 100 cubic centimeters of solution. Store this in the refrigerator until you are ready to use it. |

When you are ready to use it dilute it by 5 times. In other words put 20 cubic centimeters into a container and fill it until you have 100 cubic centimeters of diluted solution.

To make agar plates:
Dissolve 1.5 grams of agar into the solution and autoclave at 121 degrees C for 10 minutes. Cool to 55 degrees C and add 2 cc of glacial acetic acid. Allow to solidify.

Culture solution#2

2% Ca CO$_3$
0.5% Yeast extract
3% Ethyl alcohol
This is added to a 10% wort (e.g. Fleischmann's Diamalt) which is often clarified and rough filtered before the agar is added.

Hoyers solution

Combine:
(NH4)2 So4 ................................1 gram
K2HPO4.................................. 0.1 gram
KH2 PO4 ...............................0.9 grams
M g S o 4...................................0.25 grams
Ethyl alcohol 95% w/v ..................... 30 ml

Add enough distilled H2O to make 1 liter.

Beijerinks solution

Combine:
Amonium phosphate..................0.05 grams
Potassium chloride.....................0.01 grams
Absolute ethyl alcohol ...................3 grams

Add enough tap water to make 100 grams.

Pastures Nutrient

Combine:
Amonium phosphate................... 0.2 grams
Magnesium phosphate................. 0.1 grams
Calcium phosphate..................... 0.1 grams
Absolute ethyl alcohol .................. 22.50 ml
Glacial acetic acid ................... 12.75 grams

Add enough distilled water to make 1 liter.

**APPENDICES**

# FOREIGN GROWTH INHIBITORS

Yeast growth can be inhibited by the addition of 10-100 mg/ cycloheximide (Acti-dione) Mold growth can be inhibited by the addition of 10 mg/1 biphenyl.

## VINEGAR SCORE SHEET

| VINEGARS' IDENTIFICATION |
|---|
| PRODUCER |

### TEST CATEGORY

| FRUIT | GRAIN | SPIRIT |
|---|---|---|

| BLENDED<br>MIXED SUBSTRATE | BLENDED<br>MIXED VINEGAR |
|---|---|

| FLAVORED /W | OTHER |
|---|---|

### TECHNICAL NOTES

| PH | % ACID | DENSITY | @ | °F/°C |
|---|---|---|---|---|
| LIVE CULTURE | | CLARIFIED | | |
| TIME AGED | | | | |
| SUBSTRATE (S) | | | | |

## VINEGAR SCORE SHEET

| VINEGARS' IDENTIFICATION |
|---|
| PRODUCER |

### TEST CATEGORY

| FRUIT | GRAIN | SPIRIT |
|---|---|---|

| BLENDED<br>MIXED SUBSTRATE | BLENDED<br>MIXED VINEGAR |
|---|---|

| FLAVORED /W | OTHER |
|---|---|

### TECHNICAL NOTES

| PH | % ACID | DENSITY | @ | °F/°C |
|---|---|---|---|---|
| LIVE CULTURE | | CLARIFIED | | |
| TIME AGED | | | | |
| SUBSTRATE (S) | | | | |

## SCORE SHEET

**JUDGE**

|  | PTS | COMMENTS |
|---|---|---|
| PRESENTATION (0-05) |  |  |
| APPEARANCE (0-10) |  |  |
| AROMA/BOUQUET (0-25) |  |  |
| TASTE (0-25) |  |  |
| BODY/BITE (0-20) |  |  |
| AFTER TASTE (0-15) |  |  |
| TOTAL (-100) |  |  |

## VINEGAR TASTING COMMENT SHEET

VINEGAR IDENTIFICATION _____

COMMENTS_____

## SUPPLIERS OF MATERIALS APPENDIX

| VINEGAR, WINE, BEER AND OTHER ALCOHOL MAKING SUPPLIES |
| --- |
| HOME WINE AND BEER TRADE ASSOCIATION<br>DEE ROBERSON EXCUTIVE SECRETARY<br>604 NORTH MILLER ROAD<br>VALRICO FLORIDA 33594<br>USA<br>813-685-4261 |
| THESE PEOPLE WILL PUT YOU IN TOUCH WITH THE SUPPLIERS NEAREST YOU. |

| VINEGAR STARTER SOURCES |
| --- |
| Bezzola's Apple Cider Vinegar |
| Hains Apple Cider Vinegar |

# BIBLIOGRAPHY APPENDIX

Amedeo Sorentino, Natures Magic Formula, North Hollywood California ,AMI

Annenkov, M.G. The Use of Pure Cultures in the Production of Vinegar. Konsul't Brodil'noi Prom. No. 9: 24-33. 1939

Asai, Toshinobu, Acetic Acid Bacteria, University of Tokyo Press 1968

Benjamin M.Pettengill, The Manufacture of Cider and Cider Vinegar 1900

Bergey, David H. et al. Bergey's Manual of Determinative Bacteriology, The Willi,&s and Wilkins Company, Baltimore.(Always consult the latest edition since the thinking on the acetobacter is constantly changing

Botkin, C.W. and Hamiel, G.R. Spray Residue on Apples in New Mexico. K. Mex. Agr. Expt. Stn. Bul. 235. 1935

Campbell, Clyde H. Campbell's Book - Canning, Preserving, and Pickling. Vance Publishing Corporation, Chicago.Ill. 1937

Chang K.C., Food in Chinese Culture, Yale University Press

Cruess, W.V. and Joslyn, M.A. Home and Farm Preparation of Vinegar. Calif. Agr. Expt. Stn. Circ. 332.1934

Cruess, W.V. Commercial Fruit and Vegetable Products. McGraw-Hill Book Company, New York. 1945

Cruess, W.V., Zion, J.R., Sifredi, A.V. The Utility of Sulfurous Acid and Pure. Yeast in Cider Vinegar Manufacture. J. Ind.. Eng. Chem. 7: 324-3 April, 1915.

Di Baja, Atilio, Electrooligo Dynamics in the - Vinegar Industry. Anales Assoc. Quim, Argentina 31:63 1943

Di Baja, Atilio. Electrooligo Dynamics in Vinegar Manufacture. Rev. Facultad Cienc. Quim. (Argentina).1942

Eggebrecht, Hans. Banana Vinegar. Deut. Essigind. 43: 145-7.1939

Elion, H. Studien Ueber Hefe.Centralbl. F. Bakt. 14: 53-62 1893

Elmer, L.S. Vinegar Generator System. U.S. Patent 2,136,425 May 2, 1939.

Fabian, F.W. A Small Practical Vinegar Generator. Mich. Agr. Expt. SM. Circ. Bull. 174. 1941

Fabian, Frederick W. Honey Vinegar Mich, State Coll. of Agr. and Appl. Sci. Ext. October, 1933.

Fabian, Frederick, Honey Vinegar, East Lansing Agricultural Experiment Station, 1926

Fetzer, W.R, Modern Practice in Vinegar Making, Food Industries 2: 429-91.1930

Frings, H. Apparatus for Vinegar Production. U.S. Patent 2,094,592 October 3, 1937.

Frings, H. Manufacture of Vinegar, U.S. Patent 1,880,381 October 4, 1932.

Ghesquiers, Jules C. Clarifying Wines, Fr. Patent 835,530 December 23, 1935.

Haeseler, Georg. Whey Vinegar Branntweinwirtschaft Ko. 1/2, 6 pp. see Chem. Abs. 1949, 6359 g. 1947

Hansen, A.E. Making Vinegar by the Frings Process. Food Industries 7: 277, 312. 1933

Hansen, E.C, Mycoderma aceti et Mycoderma pasteuriaum Comp, Rend. 1:96.1879

Hansen, E.C, Recherches sur les Bacteries.Acetifiantes. Comp. Rend. d Lab. de Carlsberg. 3: 182-216.1993

Hansen, Maurice, Cider Vinegar, Arco 1978

Henneberg, W. Weitere Untersuchungen ueber Essigbakterien. Centralbl. F. Bakt. 4: 14-20.1898

Hildebrandt, F.M. Experinental Generator Helps in Control 1941 of Vinegar Manufacture. Food Industries 13, No. 12, 62-4.

Hopkins, R.H. , and Roberts, R.H. The Kinetics of Alcoholic Fermentation of Sugars by Brewer's Yeast, Biochem. J. 29: 919, 931, 2486.

Hopkins, R.H. and Krause, B. Biochemistry Applied to Malting and Brewing. 2nd Edition. Allen and Unnwin Ltd. London.1947

Jarvis J.C., Folk Medicine, Holt and Company, 1959

Johnson, Marsha, How to Make and Cook with Gourmet Vinegars

Kono Tomomi, Su no Fuzokushi, Tokyo: Tokyo Shobosha , 1985

Kono Tomomi, Su no Hyakka, Tokyo: Tokyo Shobosha , 1983

Lamb, A.R. and Wilson, E. Vinegar Fermentation and Home Production of Cider Vinegar. Iowa Agr. Expt. Stn. Bul. 218. 1923

Lavender, Francis Y., The Influence of Vinegar and
Concentrations of Marinades on Beef Tenderness

LeFevre, Edwin. Making Vinegar in the Home and On the Farm
U.S, Dept, Agriculture, Farmers' Bulletin. No, 1424, June,
1924,

Lowy, Joe. Automatic Control Improves Vinegar Manufacture.
Food Industries 13, No. 8,, 47-48. 1941

Manteifel, A.Y. The Use of Pure Cultures in the Production of
Vinegar. Microbiology (U.S.S.R.) 8. No, 3-4. 1941

Maurice Hanssen, Cider Vinegar, New York Arco Publishing
Co.1975

Mayer, Charles , The Manufacture of Vinegar, Wetherill,
Philadelphia 1860

Monikovskis, Casimir. Quantitative Estimation of Mycoderma
aceti in Vinegar. Mitt. Lebensm. Hyg. 31: 264-7.1940

Muller-Thurgau, In Euler's Chemic der Hefe und Alkoholische
Garung. Akademische Verlag, Leipzig.

Nixdorf, Wermer Active Vinegar. Deut. Essigind. 44: 105-6.
1940

Nixdorf, Wermer. Condensation Problems in Vinegar
Fermentation. Deut. Essigind. 41: 119-21. 1937

Pacottet Paul, Eaux-de-Vie et Vanaigres,1926, Bailliere et fils
Paris

Pasteur, Louis, Etudes Sur le Vinaigre, Paris Gauthier Villars,
1868

Prescott, S.C., and Dunn C.G. Industrial Microbiology,, 2nd Edition. McGraw-Hill Book Company, New York.1949

Robinson R. A., The Legal History of Vinegar, London Vinegar Brewers Federation 1952

Scottt, Cyril Cider Vinegar; Natures Health Promoter and Safest Treatment of Obesity London Athane publishing 1968.

Shimwell, J.L, Brewing Technology IV. The Acetic Acid Bacteria, Wallerstein Laboratories Communications. 11: 27-39 March, 1948.

The Cider Vinegar and Mollasses Recipe Book Maurice Hanssen 1976

Togo, Kuroiwa...Rice Vinegar, 1 ed. Tokyo: Kenko Igakusha

Vaughn Reese H, The Acetic Acid Bacteria, Wallerstein Laboratories Communications. 5: 5-26 April, 1942.

Vinegar; Its Manufacture and Examination, Mitchell Charles A. 1916

Vinson, A.E. Honey Vinegar Ariz, Agr. Expt. Stn. Bul. 57.1907

Williams Theadore A Practical Treatsie on the Manufacture of Vinegar and Acetates, cider and Fruit Wines, Philadelphia, H. C. Baird 1890

Wustenfeld, H. and Kreipe, H. Comparative Investigations on the Loss of Liquid in Wood and Earthenware Generators. Deut. Essigind. 41: 5-7. 1937

Wustenfeld, H. and Kreipe, H. Experiments to Determine Losses Due to Different Kinds of Generator Wood.1935

Wustenfeld, H. Lehrbuch der Essigfabrikation, Verlag. Paul Parey, Berlin.1930

Wyant, Z.N. Vinegar Mich. Agr. Coll. Expt. Stn. Bact. Section Special Bul. No. 98. November, 1919.

Ya, T. Stimulative Action of Vitamin B-1 on the Growth and Acid Fermentation of Certain Species of Vinegar Bacteria. Microbiology. 7: 841-9. 1919

# RECOMMENDED REFERENCE BOOKS APPENDIX

| WINE MAKING |
|---|

MODERN WINEMAKING------------------------------------------------------ JACKISCH
THE ART OF WINE MAKING------------------------------------------ ANDERSON
------------------------------------------------------------------------------ AND HULL
GRAPES INTO WINE------------------------------------------------------WAGNER
MAKING TABLE WINE AT HOME------------------------------------ UNIV. OF
------------------------------------------------------------------------------CALIFORNIA

| BEER MAKING |
|---|

BREWING QUALITY BEERS ----------------------------------------------------BURCH
BREWING LAGER BEERS--------------------------------------------------------NOONAN
COMPLETE JOY OF BREWING----------------------------------------PAPAZIAN

FOOTNOTES————————————————

[1]Die deutche Essigindustrie, XXX Jahrgang, Nr 1 Jan.7, 1927, Von Dr. E Huber

[2] The Role of Vinegar in Ancient Babylon, 1927, E Huber,.

[3] Vinegar: History and Development R.J. Allgeier and G.B. Nickol

[4]Assyrian Prescriptions for Diseases of the Ears, Journal of Royal Asiatic Society, 1931

[5] "Foods: The Gift of Osiris," William J. Darby, Paul Ghalioungui, Louis Grivetti, Academic Press 1977

[6] "Plinys' Natural History", Book XIV, Chapter 25, Gaius Plinus Segundus, 23-79 AD known as the elder Roman naturalist and writer.

[7]"Pliny's Natural History," Edited by J Newsome, Oxford Press

[8]"Food, The gift of Osiris"

[9]"The Jewish Encyclopedia ," Funk and Wagnal Company New York, (1906)

[10]"Jewish Encyclopedia"

[11]"Dictionary of the Bible," Volume,4 page, Pub. Charles Scribners -sons

[12]"Dictionary of the Bible"

[13] "The Pantropheon," 1977, Alexis Soyer, Paddington Press Ltd.

[14]"Food in History Reay," 1973, Tannahill, Stein and Day

[15] "Food in History Reay"

[16]"Plinys' Natural History, Book XIV, chapter 25

[17]ibid Plinys' nat. hist.

[18]ibid Plinys' nat. hist.

[19]"The Pantropheon"

[20]ibid

[21]"Alps and Elephants, Hannibals' March," Sir Gavin de Ber, F. R.S.

[22]"Food in Chinese Culture , Anthropological and Historical Perspective," 1977 K.C. Chang, Yale University Press , London

[23]"Food in Chinese Culture"

[24]"Food in Chinese Culture"

[25]"Food in Chinese Culture"

[26]"Food in Chinese Culture"

[27]"Food in Chinese Culture"

[28]"Food in Chinese Culture"

[29]"Food in Chinese Culture"

[30]"Su no Hakka (Encyclopedia of Vinegar)" 1983, Tomomi Kono Tokyo Shobo Shu

[31]"Food in History"

[32] "Food in History"

[33]"Dictionary of Gastronomy," Andre L. Simon and Robert Howe, Mc Graw Hill

# FOOTNOTES

[34] "A Taste for Change British Vinegars," 36 Park St., Croydon, Surrey CR9 1TT, London

[35] "Le Patissier Francois" 1655 ,Pierre Francois de la Varrenne

[36] "The Pantropheon"

[37] "A General Treatsie on the Manufacture of Vinegar," 1871, H. Dussauce, pub. H.C. Baird & Co Philadelphia.

[38] Modren Practice in Vinegar Making, 1930, W.R. Fetzer, Food and Industry, Vol.2 page 489

[39] The Treatment of External Otitis, 1950, I.L. Ochs, Journal of American Medical Association, Vol.142 page 1361-1362.

[40] "Folk Medicine," 1959, D.C. Jarvis, pub. Holt and Co. New York

[41] "The Pharmacological Basis of Therapeutics," A. Gilman and L.Goodman, Macmillan Publishing Company

[42] "The De Re Rustica ," 50 A.D., Columella

[43] "Forme of Curry and Ancient Cookery," 1790, pub.Warner .

[44] "The Legal History of Vinegar," 1952," by R.A. Robinson Barrister at Law and Pharmiceuticle Chemist formerly Chief Officer of the Public Control Middlesex County

[45] "Etudes Sur le Vinegre, Sa Fabrication ce Maladie Moyen de le Prevenur," 1868, Louis Pasteur

[46] Preston vs Jackson 1928, #73 solicitors journal page 712

[47] Kat vs Diment, 1950, IKB 24

[48] "The Legal History of Vinegar,"

[49] "Mycologia Europea " Vol. 42:1 pg 96, C.H. Persoon

[50] F.T. Kutzing, 1837, Journal of Practical Chemistry 11: Page 385

[51] "Memoirs sur la Fermentation Acetic", Louis Pasture, 1864, Annals of Chemistry and Physics Volume 57; page 58

[52] "Vinegar , Its Manufacture and Examination," C.A. Mitchell, 192, 2nd Edition, Charles Griffin and Company, London.

[53] "Encyclopedia of Chemical Technology," Vol. 21 page 261

[54] "Vinegar History and Development," G.B. Nichols and R.J. Allgeier

[55] Hromatka and Ebner 1949

[56] "Economic Microbiology," Acetic acid : Vinegar , R.N. Greenshields, Vol 2 Chapter 4, 1978, Academic Press

[57] A re-assessment of the of the genus acetobacter, J. L. Shimwell, Research dept., British Vinegars Limited Sommerset England, October 13,1958,

[58] Vinegar, Z.N. Wyant, Mich. Agr. Coll. Expt. Stn. Bact. Section, Special Bul. No. 95, November, 1919.

[59] Modern Practice in Vinegar Making, W.R. Fetzer, Food Industries 2: 429-91. 1930

# FOOTNOTES

[60] "Commercial Pruit and Vegetable Products," W.V. Cruess, McGraw-Hill Book Company, New York 1945

[61] "Honey Vinegar," Frederick W. Fabian, Mich, State Coll. of Agr. and Appl. Sci. Ext. October, 1933.

[62] "Lehrbuch der Essigfabrikation Verlag," H. Wustenfeld, Paul Parey , Berlin.1930

[63] Frings Information Service, Frings America Inc.

[64] Stimulative Action of Vitamin B1 on the Growth and Acid Fermentation of Certain Species of Vinegar Bacteria, T. Ya, Microbiology, 7: 941-9. 1932

[65] "Industrial Microbiology," S.C. Prescott, and C.G. Dunn, 2nd Edition. McGraw-Hill Book Company New York. 1949

[66] "Experiments to Determine Losses Due to Different Kinds of Generator Wood," H. Wustenfeld, and H. Kreipe, 1935

[67] "Experiments to Determine Losses Due to Different Kinds of Generator Wood"

[68] "Comparative Investigations on the Loss of Liquid in Wood and Earthenware Generators," H. Wustenfeld, and H. Kreipe, Deut. Essigind. 41: 5-7. 1937

[69] "Commercial Fruit and Vegetable Products," W.V. Cruess, McGraw-Hill Book Company, New York. 1945, "Home and Farm Preparation of Vinegar" W.V. Cruess, and M.A.Joslyn, Calif. Agr. Expt. Stn. Circ. 332.1934

[70] "Commercial Fruit and Vegetable Products," W.V. Cruess, McGraw-Hill Book Company, New York. 1945

[71] "Commercial Fruit and Vegetable Products," W.V. Cruess, McGraw-Hill Book Company, New York. 1945

[72] "Canning, Preserving, and Pickling,". Clyde H. Campbell, Vance Publishing Corporation, Chicago.Ill. 1937

[73] "The Utility of Sulfurous Acid and Purem Yeast in Cider Vinegar Manufacture." W.V. Cruess, J.R. Zion, A.V. Sifredi, J. Ind.. Eng. Chem. 7: 324-5 April, 1915.

[74] Ibid

[75] "Industrial Microbiology," S.C. Prescott, and C.G.Dunn , 2nd Edition. McGraw-Hill Book Company, New York.1949

[76] "The Kinetics of Alcoholic Fermentation of Sugars by Brewer's Yeast," R.H. Biochem.Hopkins, and R.H. Roberts, J. 29: 919, 931, 248. 1933

[77] "In Euler's Chemic der Hefe und Alkoholische Garung. Akademische Verlag,," Leipzig Muller-Thurgau

[78] The Acetic Acid Bacteria, Reese H. Vaughn,, Wallerstein Laboratories Commnications. 5: 5-26 April, 1942.

[79] "Home and Farm Preparation of Vinegar," W.V. Cruess, and M.A.Joslyn, Calif. Agr. Expt. Stn. Circ. 332.1934

[80] Production of Vinegar by Immobilized Cells, Process, Biochemistry June 1985, A. Mori, Tokyo Japan.

[81] My Father

# FOOTNOTES

[82] My father

[83] W.R.J. Evans, HP Foods Limited, Tower Road, Aston Cross Birmingham England

[84] The Home Book of Quotations ,Stevenson, Dodd Mead and Company

[85] "Food and Technology," R.C. Zalkan and F.W. Fabian, vol. 7 page 453 , 1953

[86] The Rarefied Relm of Aceto Balsamico, Italian Wines and Spirits, Burton Anderson, August, 1981

[87] "The American Illustrated Medical Dictionary," 20 th Edition, Dorland

[88] The Wine Spectator, S.I. Virbila, March 1-15, 1986, Page 23

[89] Natural Aceto Balsamic, Corti Brothers Sacramento Clifornia

[90] Consorzio Produttori Aceto Balsamico di Modena, The Italian Trade Commission, Rosalba Tehrani, Los Angeles,Corti Brothers, The Christian Science Monitor, The wine Spectator,and The Rarefied Relm of Aceto Balsamico, Italian Wines and Spirits, by Burton Anderson August 1981.

[91] The Wine Spectator, S.I. Virbila, March 1-15 1986, Page 23

[92] Food Processor (Australia), August 1986, page 30.

[93] Grocer (London ), August 30, 1986 page 38

[94] Milling and Baking News, October 12, 1982 Page 30.

[95] The Vinegar Encyclopedia, Tomomi Kono (Japan)

[96] Snack Food, February, 1983 Page 19

[97] New Product Promotions Trend, 16 (218) December 1985

[98] Economic Microbiology , Acetic Acid Vinegar Volume 2 Page 121,1978, Academic Press , R.N Greenshields

[99] Joyce Goldstien Chef and Owner of Square One Restaurant in San Francisco.

[100] Cider Vinegar Maurice Hansen pub. Arco 1978.

[101] Versatile Vinegar, The Vinegar Institute

[102] Versatile Vinegar, The Vinegar Institute

[103] Versatile Vinegar, The Vinegar Institute

[104] Versatile Vinegar, The Vinegar Institute

[105] Versatile Vinegar, The Vinegar Institute

[106] Versatile Vinegar, The Vinegar Institute

[107] Versatile Vinegar, The Vinegar Institute

[108] Versatile Vinegar, The Vinegar Institute

[109] Versatile Vinegar, The Vinegar Institute

[110] Versatile Vinegar, The Vinegar Institute

[111] Versatile Vinegar, The Vinegar Institute

[112] Versatile Vinegar, The Vinegar Institute

[113] Versatile Vinegar, The Vinegar Institute

# FOOTNOTES

[114]Versatile Vinegar, The Vinegar Institute

[115]Versatile Vinegar, The Vinegar Institute

[116]Organic Gardening May, 1984

[117]Versatile Vinegar, The Vinegar Institute

[118]Versatile Vinegar, The Vinegar Institute

[119]Versatile Vinegar, The Vinegar Institute

[120]Versatile Vinegar, The Vinegar Institute

[121]Versatile Vinegar, The Vinegar Institute

[122]Versatile Vinegar, The Vinegar Institute

[123]Versatile Vinegar, The Vinegar Institute

[124]Versatile Vinegar, The Vinegar Institute

[125]Versatile Vinegar, The Vinegar Institute

126U.S.Industrial Chemicals Co. Vinegar News Letter no. 30 April 15, 1960 The Medicinal Uses of Vinegar.

127U.S.Industrial Chemicals Co. Vinegar News Letter no. 30 April 15, 1960 The Medicinal Uses of Vinegar.

128 Vinegar: Building block for the Body Science Digest August 1946 John J. Oneil

129Vinegar: Building block for the Body Science Digest August 1946 John J. Oneil

130 Vinegar: Building block for the Body Science Digest August 1946 John J. Oneil

131Vinegar: Building block for the Body Science Digest August 1946 John J. Oneil

132 Treatment of External Otitis: A Simple and Effective Technique Irving L Ochs Md.Journal of the American Medical Association April 29, 1950 Volume 142 Number 17.

133 Aceti Acid Inhibition of Gram Negative Bacilli in culture Media. Journal of Bacteriology 52: 353 September 1946.

134 Treatment of External Otitis: A Simple and Effective Technique Irving L Ochs Md.Journal of the American Medical Association April 29, 1950 Volume 142 Number 17.

135Treatment of External Otitis: A Simple and Effective Technique Irving L Ochs Md.Journal of the American Medical Association April 29, 1950 Volume 142 Number 17.

136Goodman and Gilman's the Pharmacological Basis of Therapeutics Seventh Edition Macmillan Publishing Company New York Alfred G. Goodman Louis s. Goodman

137Goodman and Gilman's the Pharmacological Basis of Therapeutics Seventh Edition Macmillan Publishing Company New York Alfred G. Goodman Louis s. Goodman

138 The Genuine Works of Hippocrates Translated from the Greek by Dr.Francis Adams Surgeon Baltimore Maryland, The Williams and Wilkins Co. 1939. Hippocrates was a Greek Physician 460? to 377? B.C. Sometimes referred as the father of western medicine.

139 The American Illustrated Medical Dictionary Dorland 20th Edition pg. 1052

# FOOTNOTES

140 The Genuine Works of Hippocrates Translated from the Greek by Dr.Francis Adams Surgeon Baltimore Maryland, The Williams and Wilkins Co. 1939. pg. 76 and 77

141The Genuine Works of Hippocrates Translated from the Greek by Dr.Francis Adams Surgeon Baltimore Maryland, The Williams and Wilkins Co. 1939. pg 84

142 The Genuine Works of Hippocrates Translated from the Greek by Dr.Francis Adams Surgeon Baltimore Maryland, The Williams and Wilkins Co. 1939. pg. 277

143 The Genuine Works of Hippocrates Translated from the Greek by Dr.Francis Adams Surgeon Baltimore Maryland, The Williams and Wilkins Co. 1939. pg. 338-339

144 Chinese System of Food Cures Henry C. Lu Sterling Publishing Co. Inc. New York.

145 Chinese System of Food Cures Henry C. Lu Sterling Publishing Co. Inc. New York.

146Chinese System of Food Cures Henry C. Lu Sterling Publishing Co. Inc. New York.

147Rice Vinegar Togo Koroiwa pub.Kenko Igakusha Co. Ltd.

148U.S.Industrial Chemicals Co. Vinegar News Letter no. 30 April 15, 1960 The Medicinal Uses of Vinegar.

149Chinese System of Food Cures Henry C. Lu Sterling Publishing Co. Inc. New York.

150Chinese System of Food Cures Henry C. Lu Sterling Publishing Co. Inc. New York.

151U.S.Industrial Chemicals Co. Vinegar News Letter no. 30 April 15, 1960 The Medicinal Uses of Vinegar.

152Popular Beliefs and Superstitions, A Compendium of American Folklore by Newbell Niles Pucket Volume, G.K. Hall and Company 70 Lincoln Street Boston Mass, 1981.

153Country Remedies Karen Thesen Harper Colophon Books 1979

154Popular Beliefs and Superstitions, A Compendium of American Folklore by Newbell Niles Pucket Volume, G.K. Hall and Company 70 Lincoln Street Boston Mass, 1981.

155Popular Beliefs and Superstitions, A Compendium of American Folklore by Newbell Niles Pucket Volume, G.K. Hall and Company 70 Lincoln Street Boston Mass, 1981.

156Folk Medicine Bill Wannan Hill of Content Australia 1970

157Popular Beliefs and Superstitions, A Compendium of American Folklore by Newbell Niles Pucket Volume, G.K. Hall and Company 70 Lincoln Street Boston Mass, 1981.

158Popular Beliefs and Superstitions, A Compendium of American Folklore by Newbell Niles Pucket Volume, G.K. Hall and Company 70 Lincoln Street Boston Mass, 1981.

159Folk Medicine 19th Edition DeForest Clinton Jarvis, Henry Holt and Co. 1960

# FOOTNOTES

160Popular Beliefs and Superstitions, A Compendium of American Folklore by Newbell Niles Pucket Volume, G.K. Hall and Company 70 Lincoln Street Boston Mass, 1981.

161U.S.Industrial Chemicals Co. Vinegar News Letter no. 30 April 15, 1960 The Medicinal Uses of Vinegar.

162Popular Beliefs and Superstitions, A Compendium of American Folklore by Newbell Niles Pucket Volume, G.K. Hall and Company 70 Lincoln Street Boston Mass, 1981.

163Popular Beliefs and Superstitions, A Compendium of American Folklore by Newbell Niles Pucket Volume, G.K. Hall and Company 70 Lincoln Street Boston Mass, 1981.

164U.S.Industrial Chemicals Co. Vinegar News Letter no. 30 April 15, 1960 The Medicinal Uses of Vinegar.

165Popular Beliefs and Superstitions, A Compendium of American Folklore by Newbell Niles Pucket Volume, G.K. Hall and Company 70 Lincoln Street Boston Mass, 1981.

166Popular Beliefs and Superstitions, A Compendium of American Folklore by Newbell Niles Pucket Volume, G.K. Hall and Company 70 Lincoln Street Boston Mass, 1981.

167Popular Beliefs and Superstitions, A Compendium of American Folklore by Newbell Niles Pucket Volume, G.K. Hall and Company 70 Lincoln Street Boston Mass, 1981.

168 Folk Medicine Bill Wannan Hill of Content Australia 1970

169Popular Beliefs and Superstitions, A Compendium of American Folklore by Newbell Niles Pucket Volume, G.K. Hall and Company 70 Lincoln Street Boston Mass, 1981.

170Folk Medicine Bill Wannan Hill of Content Australia 1970

171Popular Beliefs and Superstitions, A Compendium of American Folklore by Newbell Niles Pucket Volume, G.K. Hall and Company 70 Lincoln Street Boston Mass, 1981.

172Folk Medicine Bill Wannan Hill of Content Australia 1970

173U.S.Industrial Chemicals Co. Vinegar News Letter no. 30 April 15, 1960 The Medicinal Uses of Vinegar.

174Chinese System of Food Cures Henry C. Lu Sterling Publishing Co. Inc. New York.

175Popular Beliefs and Superstitions, A Compendium of American Folklore by Newbell Niles Pucket Volume, G.K. Hall and Company 70 Lincoln Street Boston Mass, 1981.

176Popular Beliefs and Superstitions, A Compendium of American Folklore by Newbell Niles Pucket Volume, G.K. Hall and Company 70 Lincoln Street Boston Mass, 1981.

177U.S.Industrial Chemicals Co. Vinegar News Letter no. 30 April 15, 1960 The Medicinal Uses of Vinegar.

# FOOTNOTES

178Popular Beliefs and Superstitions, A Compendium of American Folklore by Newbell Niles Pucket Volume, G.K. Hall and Company 70 Lincoln Street Boston Mass, 1981.

179Chinese System of Food Cures Henry C. Lu Sterling Publishing Co. Inc. New York.

180Chinese System of Food Cures Henry C. Lu Sterling Publishing Co. Inc. New York.

181 Versatile Vinegar, The Vinegar Institute

182U.S.Industrial Chemicals Co. Vinegar News Letter no. 30 April 15, 1960 The Medicinal Uses of Vinegar.

183Popular Beliefs and Superstitions, A Compendium of American Folklore by Newbell Niles Pucket Volume, G.K. Hall and Company 70 Lincoln Street Boston Mass, 1981.

184Versatile Vinegar, The Vinegar Institute

185Popular Beliefs and Superstitions, A Compendium of American Folklore by Newbell Niles Pucket Volume, G.K. Hall and Company 70 Lincoln Street Boston Mass, 1981.

186U.S.Industrial Chemicals Co. Vinegar News Letter no. 30 April 15, 1960 The Medicinal Uses of Vinegar.

187Popular Beliefs and Superstitions, A Compendium of American Folklore by Newbell Niles Pucket Volume, G.K. Hall and Company 70 Lincoln Street Boston Mass, 1981.

188Popular Beliefs and Superstitions, A Compendium of American Folklore by Newbell Niles Pucket Volume, G.K. Hall and Company 70 Lincoln Street Boston Mass, 1981.

189Chinese System of Food Cures Henry C. Lu Sterling Publishing Co. Inc. New York.

190Country Remedies Karen Thesen Harper Colophon Books 1979

191Popular Beliefs and Superstitions, A Compendium of American Folklore by Newbell Niles Pucket Volume, G.K. Hall and Company 70 Lincoln Street Boston Mass, 1981.

192Chinese System of Food Cures Henry C. Lu Sterling Publishing Co. Inc. New York.

193Chinese System of Food Cures Henry C. Lu Sterling Publishing Co. Inc. New York.

194Chinese System of Food Cures Henry C. Lu Sterling Publishing Co. Inc. New York.

195Japanscan: Food Industry Bulletin 4 (3) May 1986 Page 6.

196Popular Beliefs and Superstitions, A Compendium of American Folklore by Newbell Niles Pucket Volume, G.K. Hall and Company 70 Lincoln Street Boston Mass, 1981

197Chinese System of Food Cures Henry C. Lu Sterling Publishing Co. Inc. New York.

# FOOTNOTES

198Popular Beliefs and Superstitions, A Compendium of American Folklore by Newbell Niles Pucket Volume, G.K. Hall and Company 70 Lincoln Street Boston Mass, 1981.

199Popular Beliefs and Superstitions, A Compendium of American Folklore by Newbell Niles Pucket Volume, G.K. Hall and Company 70 Lincoln Street Boston Mass, 1981.

200Chinese System of Food Cures Henry C. Lu Sterling Publishing Co. Inc. New York.

201U.S.Industrial Chemicals Co. Vinegar News Letter no. 30 April 15, 1960 The Medicinal Uses of Vinegar.

202Popular Beliefs and Superstitions, A Compendium of American Folklore by Newbell Niles Pucket Volume, G.K. Hall and Company 70 Lincoln Street Boston Mass, 1981.

203Popular Beliefs and Superstitions, A Compendium of American Folklore by Newbell Niles Pucket Volume, G.K. Hall and Company 70 Lincoln Street Boston Mass, 1981.

204Popular Beliefs and Superstitions, A Compendium of American Folklore by Newbell Niles Pucket Volume, G.K. Hall and Company 70 Lincoln Street Boston Mass, 1981.

205Popular Beliefs and Superstitions, A Compendium of American Folklore by Newbell Niles Pucket Volume, G.K. Hall and Company 70 Lincoln Street Boston Mass, 1981.

206Chinese System of Food Cures Henry C. Lu Sterling Publishing Co. Inc. New York.

207Chinese System of Food Cures Henry C. Lu Sterling Publishing Co. Inc. New York.

208Popular Beliefs and Superstitions, A Compendium of American Folklore by Newbell Niles Pucket Volume, G.K. Hall and Company 70 Lincoln Street Boston Mass, 1981.

209U.S.Industrial Chemicals Co. Vinegar News Letter no. 30 April 15, 1960 The Medicinal Uses of Vinegar.

210Popular Beliefs and Superstitions, A Compendium of American Folklore by Newbell Niles Pucket Volume, G.K. Hall and Company 70 Lincoln Street Boston Mass, 1981.

211U.S.Industrial Chemicals Co. Vinegar News Letter no. 30 April 15, 1960 The Medicinal Uses of Vinegar.

212U.S.Industrial Chemicals Co. Vinegar News Letter no. 30 April 15, 1960 The Medicinal Uses of Vinegar.

213Popular Beliefs and Superstitions, A Compendium of American Folklore by Newbell Niles Pucket Volume, G.K. Hall and Company 70 Lincoln Street Boston Mass, 1981.

214Folk Medicine 19th Edition DeForest Clinton Jarvis, Henry Holt and Co. 1960

215Popular Beliefs and Superstitions, A Compendium of American Folklore by Newbell Niles Pucket Volume, G.K. Hall and Company 70 Lincoln Street Boston Mass, 1981.

# FOOTNOTES

216Popular Beliefs and Superstitions, A Compendium of American Folklore by Newbell Niles Pucket Volume, G.K. Hall and Company 70 Lincoln Street Boston Mass, 1981.

217Popular Beliefs and Superstitions, A Compendium of American Folklore by Newbell Niles Pucket Volume, G.K. Hall and Company 70 Lincoln Street Boston Mass, 1981.

218Folk Medicine Bill Wannan Hill of Content Australia 1970

219U.S.Industrial Chemicals Co. Vinegar News Letter no. 30 April 15, 1960 The Medicinal Uses of Vinegar.

220Popular Beliefs and Superstitions, A Compendium of American Folklore by Newbell Niles Pucket Volume, G.K. Hall and Company 70 Lincoln Street Boston Mass, 1981.

221Folk Medicine 19th Edition DeForest Clinton Jarvis, Henry Holt and Co. 1960

222Popular Beliefs and Superstitions, A Compendium of American Folklore by Newbell Niles Pucket Volume, G.K. Hall and Company 70 Lincoln Street Boston Mass, 1981.

223Popular Beliefs and Superstitions, A Compendium of American Folklore by Newbell Niles Pucket Volume, G.K. Hall and Company 70 Lincoln Street Boston Mass, 1981.

224U.S.Industrial Chemicals Co. Vinegar News Letter no. 30 April 15, 1960 The Medicinal Uses of Vinegar.

225Folk Medicine Bill Wannan Hill of Content Australia 1970

226Folk Medicine 19th Edition DeForest Clinton Jarvis, Henry Holt and Co. 1960

227Chinese System of Food Cures Henry C. Lu Sterling Publishing Co. Inc. New York.

228United States Patent 3,949.067

229Folk Medicine 19th Edition DeForest Clinton Jarvis, Henry Holt and Co. 1960

230U.S.Industrial Chemicals Co. Vinegar News Letter no. 30 April 15, 1960 The Medicinal Uses of Vinegar.

231Country Remedies Karen Thesen Harper Colophon Books 1979

232Popular Beliefs and Superstitions, A Compendium of American Folklore by Newbell Niles Pucket Volume, G.K. Hall and Company 70 Lincoln Street Boston Mass, 1981.

233Popular Beliefs and Superstitions, A Compendium of American Folklore by Newbell Niles Pucket Volume, G.K. Hall and Company 70 Lincoln Street Boston Mass, 1981.

234U.S.Industrial Chemicals Co. Vinegar News Letter no. 30 April 15, 1960 The Medicinal Uses of Vinegar.

235U.S.Industrial Chemicals Co. Vinegar News Letter no. 30 April 15, 1960 The Medicinal Uses of Vinegar.

236Folk Medicine Bill Wannan Hill of Content Australia 1970

237Country Remedies Karen Thesen Harper Colophon Books 1979

238Popular Beliefs and Superstitions, A Compendium of American Folklore by Newbell Niles Pucket Volume, G.K. Hall and Company 70 Lincoln Street Boston Mass, 1981.

# FOOTNOTES

239Popular Beliefs and Superstitions, A Compendium of American Folklore by Newbell Niles Pucket Volume, G.K. Hall and Company 70 Lincoln Street Boston Mass, 1981.

240Popular Beliefs and Superstitions, A Compendium of American Folklore by Newbell Niles Pucket Volume, G.K. Hall and Company 70 Lincoln Street Boston Mass, 1981.

241Popular Beliefs and Superstitions, A Compendium of American Folklore by Newbell Niles Pucket Volume, G.K. Hall and Company 70 Lincoln Street Boston Mass, 1981.

242Popular Beliefs and Superstitions, A Compendium of American Folklore by Newbell Niles Pucket Volume, G.K. Hall and Company 70 Lincoln Street Boston Mass, 1981.

243Popular Beliefs and Superstitions, A Compendium of American Folklore by Newbell Niles Pucket Volume, G.K. Hall and Company 70 Lincoln Street Boston Mass, 1981.

244 A Minnesota Doctors Home Remedies for Common and Uncommon Ailments John Eichenlaub M.D. Prentice Hall Inc 1972.

245The Practical art of Medicine Robert B. Taylor Harper and Row 1972

246Folk Medicine 19th Edition DeForest Clinton Jarvis, Henry Holt and Co. 1960

247Popular Beliefs and Superstitions, A Compendium of American Folklore by Newbell Niles Pucket Volume, G.K. Hall and Company 70 Lincoln Street Boston Mass, 1981.

248Folk Medicine Bill Wannan Hill of Content Australia 1970 from Topsels History of Four Footed Beast

249Popular Beliefs and Superstitions, A Compendium of American Folklore by Newbell Niles Pucket Volume, G.K. Hall and Company 70 Lincoln Street Boston Mass, 1981.

250Popular Beliefs and Superstitions, A Compendium of American Folklore by Newbell Niles Pucket Volume, G.K. Hall and Company 70 Lincoln Street Boston Mass, 1981.

251Popular Beliefs and Superstitions, A Compendium of American Folklore by Newbell Niles Pucket Volume, G.K. Hall and Company 70 Lincoln Street Boston Mass, 1981.

252Lessons from My Father

253Cider Vinegar Maurice Hansen Arco Publishing Co. New York 1978

254Cider Vinegar Maurice Hansen Arco Publishing Co. New York 1978

255Cider Vinegar Maurice Hansen Arco Publishing Co. New York 1978

256Cider Vinegar Maurice Hansen Arco Publishing Co. New York 1978

257Cider Vinegar Maurice Hansen Arco Publishing Co. New York 1978

258Popular Beliefs and Superstitions, A Compendium of American Folklore by Newbell Niles Pucket Volume, G.K. Hall and Company 70 Lincoln Street Boston Mass, 1981.

259Cider Vinegar Maurice Hansen Arco Publishing Co. New York 1978

# FOOTNOTES

[260]Cider Vinegar Maurice Hansen Arco Publishing Co. New York 1978
[261]Versatile Vinegar, The Vinegar Institute
[262]Cider Vinegar Maurice Hansen Arco Publishing Co. New York 1978
[263]"Vinegar: It's Manufacture and Examination," C.A. Mitchell
[264]Versatile Vinegar, The Vinegar Institute, P.O. Box 720215, Atlanta, Georgia
[265]Versatile Vinegar, The Vinegar Institute
[266]Versatile Vinegar, The Vinegar Institute
[267]Versatile Vinegar, The Vinegar Institute
[268]Versatile Vinegar, The Vinegar Institute
[269]Versatile Vinegar, The Vinegar Institute
[270]Versatile Vinegar, The Vinegar Institute
[271]Versatile Vinegar, The Vinegar Institute
[272]Versatile Vinegar, The Vinegar Institute
[273]Versatile Vinegar, The Vinegar Institute
[274]Versatile Vinegar, The Vinegar Institute
[275]Versatile Vinegar, The Vinegar Institute
[276] Versatile Vinegar, The Vinegar Institute
[277]Versatile Vinegar, The Vinegar Institute
[278]Versatile Vinegar, The Vinegar Institute
[279]Versatile Vinegar, The Vinegar Institute
[280]Versatile Vinegar, The Vinegar Institute, P.O. Box 720215, Atlanta, Georgia
[281]Versatile Vinegar, The Vinegar Institute
[282]Versatile Vinegar, The Vinegar Institute
[283]Versatile Vinegar, The Vinegar Institute
[284]Versatile Vinegar, The Vinegar Institute
[285]Versatile Vinegar, The Vinegar Institute
[286]Versatile Vinegar, The Vinegar Institute
[287]Versatile Vinegar, The Vinegar Institute
[288]Versatile Vinegar, The Vinegar Institute
[289]Versatile Vinegar, The Vinegar Institute
[290]Versatile Vinegar, The Vinegar Institute
[291]Versatile Vinegar, The Vinegar Institute
[292]Versatile Vinegar, The Vinegar Institute
[293]Versatile Vinegar, The Vinegar Institute
[294]Versatile Vinegar, The Vinegar Institute
[295]Versatile Vinegar, The Vinegar Institute
[296]Versatile Vinegar, The Vinegar Institute

# FOOTNOTES

[297] Versatile Vinegar, The Vinegar Institute

[298] Versatile Vinegar, The Vinegar Institute

[299] Versatile Vinegar, The Vinegar Institute

[300] Versatile Vinegar, The Vinegar Institute

[301] Versatile Vinegar, The Vinegar Institute

[302] Versatile Vinegar, The Vinegar Institute

[303] Versatile Vinegar, The Vinegar Institute

[304] "The Heinze Vinegar Almanac," Heinze U.S.A., P.O. Box 57, Pittsburgh, PA 15230

[305] Versatile Vinegar, The Vinegar Institute

[306] Versatile Vinegar, The Vinegar Institute

[307] Versatile Vinegar, The Vinegar Institute

[308] Versatile Vinegar, The Vinegar Institute

[309] Versatile Vinegar, The Vinegar Institute

[310] Versatile Vinegar, The Vinegar Institute

[311] Versatile Vinegar, The Vinegar Institute

[312] Versatile Vinegar, The Vinegar Institute

[313] Authors Experiment but no claim for originality is made

[314] Versatile Vinegar, The Vinegar Institute

[315] Versatile Vinegar, The Vinegar Institute

[316] Versatile Vinegar, The Vinegar Institute

[317] Versatile Vinegar, The Vinegar Institute, P.O. Box 720215, Atlanta, Georgia

[318] Versatile Vinegar, The Vinegar Institute

[319] Versatile Vinegar, The Vinegar Institute

[320] Versatile Vinegar, The Vinegar Institute

[321] Versatile Vinegar, The Vinegar Institute

[322] Versatile Vinegar, The Vinegar Institute

[323] Versatile Vinegar, The Vinegar Institute

[324] Versatile Vinegar, The Vinegar Institute

[325] Versatile Vinegar, The Vinegar Institute

[326] Versatile Vinegar, The Vinegar Institute

[327] Versatile Vinegar, The Vinegar Institute

[328] Versatile Vinegar, The Vinegar Institute

[329] Versatile Vinegar, The Vinegar Institute

[330] Versatile Vinegar, The Vinegar Institute

[331] Versatile Vinegar, The Vinegar Institute

[332] Dictionary of Mythology Folklore and Symbols Volume 2 page 1651 (1962) Gertrude Jobes Scarecrow Press

# FOOTNOTES

[333]"Popular Beliefs and Superstitions", A Compendium of American Folklore by Newbell Niles Pucket Volume, G.K. Hall and Company 70 Lincoln Street Boston Mass, 1981.

[334]"Popular Beliefs and Superstitions", A Compendium of American Folklore by Newbell Niles Pucket Volume, G.K. Hall and Company 70 Lincoln Street Boston Mass, 1981.

[335]"Popular Beliefs and Superstitions", A Compendium of American Folklore by Newbell Niles Pucket Volume, G.K. Hall and Company 70 Lincoln Street Boston Mass, 1981.

[336]"Popular Beliefs and Superstitions", A Compendium of American Folklore by Newbell Niles Pucket Volume, G.K. Hall and Company 70 Lincoln Street Boston Mass, 1981.

[337]"Popular Beliefs and Superstitions", A Compendium of American Folklore by Newbell Niles Pucket Volume, G.K. Hall and Company 70 Lincoln Street Boston Mass, 1981.

[338]"Popular Beliefs and Superstitions", A Compendium of American Folklore by Newbell Niles Pucket Volume, G.K. Hall and Company 70 Lincoln Street Boston Mass, 1981.

[339]"Popular Beliefs and Superstitions", A Compendium of American Folklore by Newbell Niles Pucket Volume, G.K. Hall and Company 70 Lincoln Street Boston Mass, 1981.

[340]"Popular Beliefs and Superstitions", A Compendium of American Folklore by Newbell Niles Pucket Volume, G.K. Hall and Company 70 Lincoln Street Boston Mass, 1981.

[341]"Popular Beliefs and Superstitions", A Compendium of American Folklore by Newbell Niles Pucket Volume, G.K. Hall and Company 70 Lincoln Street Boston Mass, 1981.

[342]"Popular Beliefs and Superstitions", A Compendium of American Folklore by Newbell Niles Pucket Volume, G.K. Hall and Company 70 Lincoln Street Boston Mass, 1981.

[343]"Popular Beliefs and Superstitions", A Compendium of American Folklore by Newbell Niles Pucket Volume, G.K. Hall and Company 70 Lincoln Street Boston Mass, 1981.

[344]"Popular Beliefs and Superstitions", A Compendium of American Folklore by Newbell Niles Pucket Volume, G.K. Hall and Company 70 Lincoln Street Boston Mass, 1981.

[345]The Home Book of Proverbs, Maxims and Familiar Quotations, Stevenson

[346]The Home Book of Quotations, Stevenson,  Dodd Mead and Company

[347]The Oxford diet of Quotations 3rd edition

[348]The International Thesaurus of Quotations, Rhoda  T. Tripp

[349]The Home Book of Quotations ,Stevenson, Dodd Mead and Company

# FOOTNOTES

350 The Oxford diet of Quotations 3rd edition

351 The Home Book of Quotations ,Stevenson, Dodd Mead and Company

352 The Home Book of Quotations ,Stevenson, Dodd Mead and Company

353 Jewish Encyclopedia

354 Jewish Encyclopedia

355 The Home Book of Proverbs, Maxims and Familiar Quotations, Stevenson

356 Jewish Encyclopedia

357 The Oxford diet of Quotations 3rd edition

358 The Oxford diet of Quotations 3rd edition

359 The Home Book of Proverbs, Maxims and Familiar Quotations, Stevenson

360 The Home Book of Proverbs, Maxims and Familiar Quotations, Stevenson

361 Concise dictionary of 26 Languages  Peter M. Bergman

362 Concise dictionary of 26 Languages  Peter M. Bergman

363 Concise dictionary of 26 Languages  Peter M. Bergman

364 Concise dictionary of 26 Languages  Peter M. Bergman

365 Concise dictionary of 26 Languages  Peter M. Bergman

366 Concise dictionary of 26 Languages  Peter M. Bergman

367 Concise dictionary of 26 Languages  Peter M. Bergman

368 Concise dictionary of 26 Languages  Peter M. Bergman

369 Concise dictionary of 26 Languages  Peter M. Bergman

370 Concise dictionary of 26 Languages  Peter M. Bergman

371 Concise dictionary of 26 Languages  Peter M. Bergman

372 Concise dictionary of 26 Languages  Peter M. Bergman

373 Concise dictionary of 26 Languages  Peter M. Bergman

374 Concise dictionary of 26 Languages  Peter M. Bergman

375 Concise dictionary of 26 Languages  Peter M. Bergman

376 Concise dictionary of 26 Languages  Peter M. Bergman

377 Concise dictionary of 26 Languages  Peter M. Bergman

378 Concise dictionary of 26 Languages  Peter M. Bergman

379 Concise dictionary of 26 Languages  Peter M. Bergman

380 Authors father

381 1934 Cruess, W.V. and Joslyn, M.A. Home and Farm Preparation of Vinegar. Calif. Agr. Expt. Stn. Circ. 332.

382 Making Vinegar in the Home and on the Farm United States Dept. of Agriculture Edwin Lefevre Farm Bulletin 1424

# FOOTNOTES

[383] 1945 Cruess, W.V. Commercial Fruit and Vegetable Products. McGraw-Hill Book Company, New York.

[384] Ibid

[385] 1939 Eggebrecht, Hans. Banana Vinegar. Deut. Essigind. 43: 147-7

[386] 1944 Ramirez, Jose. Puerto Rico Ought to Produce Vinegar for Industrial and Domestic Uses .Rev. Agr. Ind. y Com. (Puerto Rico).33: 179-83.

[387] Ibid

[388] Ibid

[389] 1945 Cruess, W.V. Commercial Fruit and Vegetable Products. McGraw-Hill Book Company, New York.

[390] Harvey T. Chan  Handbook of Tropical Foods, Marcel Dekker Inc. 1983 U.S.A.

[391] Ibid

[392] Ibid

[393] Wyant, Z.N. Vinegar Mich. Agr. Coll. Expt. Stn. Bact. Section Special Bul. No. 98. November, 1919.

[394] (61)   Vinson, A.E. Honey Vinegar Ariz, Agr. Expt. Stn. Bul. 57.1907

[395] Fabian, Frederick W. Honey Vinegar Mich, State Coll. of Agr. and Appl. Sci. Ext. October, 1933.

[396] Wustenfeld, H. Lehrbuch der Essigfabrikation, Verlag. Paul Parey, Berlin.1930

[397] Haeseler, Georg. Whey Vinegar Branntweinwirtschaft Ko. 1/2, 6 pp. see Chem. Abs. 1949, 6359g. 1947

[398] Economic Microbiology , Volume 2 1978 , Academic Press , R.N Greenshields

[399] Economic Microbiology , Volume 2 1978 , Academic Press , R.N Greenshields

[400] Economic Microbiology , Volume 2 1978 , Academic Press , R.N Greenshields

[401] Economic Microbiology , Volume 2 1978 , Academic Press , R.N Greenshields

# INDEX

# INDEX

# INDEX

# INDEX

# INDEX

THE UNIVERSE IS PERFECT
THE ALL SEEING, ALL KNOWING , ALMIGHTY
CREATOR
DOES NOT MAKE MISTAKES

ALL  PRAISE  TO  THE  ALMIGHTY

Printed in the United States
117389LV00001B/265/A